투어 에스코트 영어

배 찬 · 김 정 욱 공저

남두도서

남두(南斗) : 남두육성(南斗六星)

은하의 중심인 사수자리에 있는 국자모양의 여섯 개의 별로서, 인간의 탄생을 결정하는 별로 알려져 있다.

머 리 말

21세기는 국경 없는 지구촌시대라 하여 국제화 및 지구촌화 추세에 발맞추어 세계의 인구는 대량으로 이동을 하며, 해외여행 완전자유화로 인하여 관광현상에 있어서는 더더욱 그리하게 되었다. 그로 인하여 세계인들과의 만남도 빈번해지게 되었다. 이제 관광은 현대인들의 삶의 일부가 되었으며, 많은 사람들의 해외여행에 유용하고 다양한 정보를 제공하며 편안한 여행이 될 수 있도록 도와주는 국외여행 인솔자는 그 나라를 대표하는 민간 외교관 또는 국가 홍보요원이라 할 수 있다. 그러므로 국외여행 인솔자는 무엇보다도 업무수행에 필요한 전문지식뿐 아니라 유창한 외국어 실력이 필요하다 하겠다. 따라서 이 책은 이러한 국외여행 인솔자들에게 필요한 여러 사항들을 순차적으로 나열하였다.

이 책은 전체 8장으로 구성되어 있는데, 제1장에서는 출발부터 도착까지 사용되는 여러 사항들인 비자와 여권 발급에서부터 항공권 구입과 출국수속을 거쳐 기내와 입국수속에 사용되는 회화들을 순차적으로 나열하였다. 제2장에서는 공항에서 호텔로 가는 중에 사용되는 가이드와의 미팅에서부터 렌터카 이용에 관한 국외여행 인솔자의 역할을 자세하게 나열하고 있다. 제3장에서는 호텔예약에서부터 체크인, 객실에서의 전화·룸·세탁 서비스 등의 각종 서비스에 관한 내용에서부터 체크아웃에 대한 영어회화를 구체적으로 나누어 구성하였다. 제4장에서는 관광지 선택과 쇼핑에 대한 영어회화를 여러 상황으로 구분하였다. 제5장에서는 공장 견학과 연극·영화 티켓 예매에 대하여 나열하였다. 제6장에서는 레스토랑과 바에서의 예약과 주문, 그리고 계산에 관련된 회화들로 이루어졌다. 제7장에서는 항공기에서 일어날 수 있는 문제에서부터 분실·사고 등의 각종 문제 처리에 대한 내용들로 구성하였다. 제8장에서는 우체국과 은행에서 사용되는 회화들로 나열하였다. 또한 이 책에서는 우리와는 기본적으로 다른 미국의 행동양식을 이해하고 그로 인하여 자연스런 인간관계가 가능하도록 미국의 관습과 미신에 대한 설명을 첨가하였다.

이 책은 여행에서 이루어질 수 있는 모든 상황들을 정해진 순서대로 일목요연하게 정리하였으나 미비한 점은 지속적으로 수정하고 보완할 것을 약속드린다. 여러 가지로 부족하지만 국외여행 인솔 업무를 학습하는 학생들이나 현장에서 종사하는 종사자들이 이 책을 통하여 많은 도움을 얻고, 또한 유용한 지침서가 되기를 희망한다.

끝으로 늘 훌륭한 책을 출판하시며 이 책의 출판될 수 있도록 물심양면으로 지원을 해주신 남두도서의 남승우 사장님과 편집부 직원 여러분들께도 깊은 감사의 마음을 전합니다.

저자 올림

차 례

Chapter 1

출발에서 도착까지

여기에서는 한국발 북미행의 경우를 설정하고 있다. 한국발 항공기에는 한국어를 하는 승무원이 탑승하고 있고, 기내에서 외국어는 필요하지는 않지만 해외여행 중에 기내에서의 외국어 회화가 전혀 필요 없을 리는 없고, 탑승편의 재확인이라도 필요하다고 할 수 있다. 실제로 귀국편의 탑승 등에서는 필요하게 된다.

승객이 항공여행을 하고자 공항에 나오는 경우 CIQ 내의 제반수속을 거쳐서 항공기에 탑승하게 된다. 따라서 승객이 체크인(check-in)에 필요한 항공권은 물론 여권, 비자, 출국신고서, 검역증 등의 여행 구비서류를 갖추었는지 인솔자는 확인해야 한다.

탑승편의 재확인

출발 전에 출발 예정지의 체재가 3일 이상일 경우에는 반드시 그 예정편의 예약을 재확인하는 것이 필요하다. 탑승편의 재확인에는 탑승편명, 탑승일시, 목적지, 예약의 유무, 단체명, 체크인 공항명, 출발시간, 기내식 등을 체크한다.

탑승 신고 및 출입국 신고서 작성

체크인 카운터에서 탑승 수속을 하는 여행객의 경우에는 먼저 해당 항공사에서 운영하는 체크인 카운터로 이동하여 탑승 수속을 받고, 체크인 카운터에서는 기내의 휴대하는 물품을 제외하고는 모두 위탁 수하물로 처리하여야 한다.

체크인 카운터에 비치된 출입국 신고서를 작성하여 출국 신고시 제출한다. 출입국 신고서는 출국장 안에도 비치되어 있으나, 인솔자가 미리 작성해두는 것이 편리하며, 출국 수속시간을 단축할 수 있다.

탑 승

탑승구에는 항공사 직원이 승객의 탑승권을 확인한 후 그 일부를 수거하여 출입국 관리사무소에 수거된 출입국 카드 수와 일치되면 출항허가를 얻게 된다. 기내에서 국외여행 인솔자의 임무는 단원 전체의 질문과 요구를 승무원에게 틀림없이 전달할 수 있어야 하고, 기내방송과 승무원으로부터의 메시지를 단원에게 전부 알릴 필요가 있다.

좌석 배정

개인별 · 단체별로 선호하는 바에 따라 또는 항공기의 탑재관리를 고려하는 일정 원칙에 따라 좌석의 배정을 받게 된다.

기내 서비스

여행객이 좌석에 앉으면 좌석 배정표와 대조하면서 전원이 착석했는지를 체크한다. 그러나 기내에서의 여행객을 돕는 것은 객실 승무원의 일이기 때문에 인솔자는 필요 이상으로는 나서지 말아야 한다.

기내에 들어가면 승무원에게 자신이 인솔자임을 알리고, 기내식이 나오는 시각 및 영화의 유무 등을 사전에 알아두어야 한다.

항공기가 이륙해서 수평비행에 들어가서 벨트 착용 사인이 꺼지고 나면 안내원은 그때에 고객의 좌석을 한바퀴 돌아본다. 좌석을 눕히는 방법이라든지, 통풍구, 독서등, 콜버튼 이용법, 화장실의 위치 등을 설명해주면 된다. 장시간 앉아 있으면 피곤하므로 고객들이 상의를 벗거나, 슬리퍼로 갈아 신거나, 좌석을 뉘어서 잠을 청하거나 등 편하게 쉬도록 배려한다.

입국에 필요한 서류가 있다면 승무원에게 미리 전달받아 고객들에게 나누어 주고 작성하도록 한다.

입국절차

검역은 문제가 일어날 일은 우선 없다. 통관에는 세관담당자와 단원과의 대화를 원만하게 처리하는 능력이 필요하다.

기내에서 승무원이 나누어주는 입국신고서를 비행기 안에서 미리 작성하면 입국수속을 편리하고 신속하게 할 수 있는데, 인솔자가 미리 작성해두면 좋다.

입국수속을 하는 창구가 자국민과 외국인으로 구분되어 실시하는 곳도 있으므로 줄을 정확히 서야 하며, 체재예정일 수를 묻기도 하고, 항공권의 제시를 요구하기도 하므로 인솔자가 선두에 서서 필요에 따라 입국심사관을 거들어준다. 이때 항공권은 각자에게 나누어주고 입국수속이 끝난 다음 회수하도록 한다.

세관 신고물품이 없는 경우 '여행자 휴대품 신고서'를 제출할 필요 없이 그대로 통과하면 된다.

포터의 이용

단체로 통관할 수 있는 곳에서는 포터를 불러 수하물 총수와 클레임 택의 특징을 말하고, 전원의 수하물을 한 곳에 모은다. 전원의 수하물을 모은 시점에서 인솔자는 개수를 반복해서 확인하고, 여행객들에게도 자신의 수하물이 틀림없는가를 확인하도록 한다. 그 후 전원의 짐을 포터에게 운반하도록 하고, 인솔자는 단체를 유도하면서 통관을 마치도록 한다. 이 경우에 수하물을 거의 검사하지 않는 것이 보통이다.

마중나온 현지 수배대리점의 직원이 세관역 내까지 들어올 수 있는 국가에서는 그 직원이 포터를 부르거나 통관을 돕기 때문에 업무는 매우 편하게 된다. 단지 수하물의 확인만은 타인에게 맡기지 말고 반드시 인솔자가 하도록 한다. 세관역 내의 출입이 금지된 국가에서는 포터에게 수하물을 운반시킬 때 현지 여행사나 마중 나온 버스회사의 이름을 말해둔다.

수하물은 수하물차로 운반하는 것이 통상적이지만 포터에게 전부 맡기고 마음대로 수하물에 손을 대면 포터의 업무방해가 된다. 어쩔 수 없이 수하물차를 사용하고 싶을 때는 포터의 양해를 구하는 것이 필요하다.

1 탑승 전까지의 전반적인 사항들

(1) 항공권 이용에 대한 전반적인 회화

1) 비자 신청(A)

T : Traveler	E : Embassy Officer

E : May I help you?

T : I'd like to apply for a visa.

E : Could you answer a few questions?

T : Of course.

E : When and where were you born?

T : I was born on January 10, 1970 in Seoul.

E : Could you tell me what is your purpose in applying for a visa?

T : I'm going on a trip to New York.

E : How long will you be staying in the New York?

T : For a month.

E : Please fill out this form and hand it in with a photo. And you can pick up your visa anytime after 10 a.m. on Friday.

T : OK. Thank you.

2) 비자 신청(B)

T : Traveler	**E :** Embassy Officer

T : I'd like to extend my visa for the United States.

E : Can you tell me what you're applying for?

T : For attending the research project of the University in Washington, D.C.

E : How long do you expect to stay?

T : For six weeks.

E : Your visa has been approved. This visa is good for 10 years.

T : Thank you.

[그림 1] 대한민국 여권 및 미국 비자 견본

3) 항공편 예약(A)

T : Tour Conductor　　　**A :** Airline's Staff

A : American Airlines. May I help you?

T : Yes, I'm a tour conductor. I'd like to make a reservation for a flight seat 30 to New York.

A : Would that be a round-trip ticket or one-way?

T : Round-trip, please.

A: When would you like to leave?

T: On next Monday. Do you have any evening flight?

A: Hold on, please. I'll check to see if there's room. (in a while) That's fine.

T: Oh, good.

A: There are three fights, one at 6:30 p.m. another at 9 p.m. and the other at 11 p.m. Which one would you like to make, sir?

T: I'd like to take the 6:30 p.m. flight. What's the fare?

A: What class would you like?

T: I'd like to reserve an economy class seat, please.

A: All right. It's 700 dollars for round-trip. May I have your name and telephone number?

T: My name is Kim. My phone number is 02-565-6482.

A: OK. Your reservation is made for flight AA 210 leaving for New York, next Monday at 6:30 p.m. We'll contact you if there are any changes in the flight time.

T: That's all right. And where and when can I pick up the ticket?

E: You can pick up your ticket at your convenience and American Airlines desk at the airport.

T: OK. Can I pay by credit card?

E: Of course, sir. We accept any credit card.

T: Very well. Thank you so much.

E: It's my pleasure. And thank you for your calling to reserve.

4) 항공편 예약(B)

T: Tour Conductor	**A:** Airline's Staff

A: American Airlines, Sue speaking. How can I help you?

T: Do you have any flights available to Las Vegas?

A: Yes, we have.

T: Is that a nonstop flight?

A: No, it flies to Las Vegas via Tokyo.

T: How often are there flights to Las Vegas?

A: There are four flights, at 8 a.m. What time shall I make your reservation for?

T: I'd like to fly at 5 p.m.

A: What class would you like?

T: I'd like to reserve an business class seat, and round-trip, please.

A: All right, and thank you for flying American Airlines.

5) 항공편 예약(C)

T: Tour Conductor	**A:** Airline's Staff

A: American Airlines. May I help you?

T: Do you have any direct flights to San Francisco?

A: Yes, sir.

T: How often do you have flights to San Francisco.

A: Every three hours between 6 a.m. and 12 a.m. When for?

T: March 12th.

A: I'm afraid there are no seats available on that flight.

What date do you want your return flight?

T: March 19th.

A: The only thing available on march 13th is flight at 9 p.m.

T: No, it's late. Then put me on your waiting list for March 12th, please.

A: Sure, if there is any cancellation for March 12th, we'll call you.

T: OK, thank you a lot.

6) 항공편 예약(D)

T: Tour Conductor	**A:** Airline's Staff

T: What time do you have night flights to Hawaii?

A: We have a flight leaving at 8 p.m.

T: How long does the flight take?

A: It takes 5 hours.

T: What's the fare for a round-trip and economy class?

A: It's $ 420, sir.

T: Do you have any cheaper tickets?

A: Yes, we have only ticket cheaper than this. But it files to Hawaii via Guam. It takes 10 hours.

T: OK, I'll take it.

7) 항공편 예약(E)

T: Tour Conductor	**A:** Airline's Staff

A: Good morning. Thank you for calling American Airlines. Can I help you?

T: Yes, I want to fly to New York on Sunday morning, January 25. Do you have a flight to New York on that morning?

A: Yes, we do. We have flights departing at 11 a.m. and 8 p.m.

T: Is that a nonstop flight?

A: No. There's a one-hour stop for refueling in Anchorage.

T: Well, one hour isn't so bad.

A: No. You still get to New York in the morning.

T: OK. I'd like to reserve an economy class seat on the 11 a.m. flight. Do you have space available?

A: Yes, I think we do. Let me check on that for you.

T: Would you, please?

A: We have space in economy class.

T: Good. What's the economy class fare to New York?

A: 505 dollars.

T: What's the difference between the economy and first class fare?

A: Well, the first class fare is 720 dollars.

T: I'd like to reserve an economy class seat. Which airport does the 11 a.m. flight leave from?

A: LA International.

T: Can I pick up my ticket there?

A: Yes, but please check in at least 1 hour before departure time.

(2) 탑승편의 재확인

1) 전화로 탑승편 확인(A)

T : Tour Conductor	**A :** Airline's Staff

A : American Airlines. May I help you?

T : I'd like to confirm my reservation.

A : Would you tell me your name and flight number, sir?

T : My name is Kim, the flight number is AA 210 for New York on next Monday.

A : Just a minute, please. Let me check you reservation. Oh, your reservation is confirmed in economy class.

T : OK. What time should I be at the airport?

A : You should be at the airport at least two hours before departure. And your boarding time is 6:00 p.m.

T : How many carry-on bags am I allowed?

A : We allow only one carry-on, which has to fit under the seat.

T: OK. Thank you so much.

2) 전화로 탑승편 확인(B)

T: Tour Conductor	**A:** Airline's Staff

A: Hello, This is American Airlines, Group desk.

T: Hello, I'd like to reconfirm reservations for our party of 30 people in all.

A: May I ask the name of your group?

T: It could be under Happy Tour.

A: Hold on, please. Let me see. Yes, 30 seats are now confirmed on flight 271 to Philadelpia this wednesday evening. May I ask your name and phone number?

T: I'm at Ritz Hotel. Phone number is 714-576-2878. My name is Kim.

A: OK, you have to arrive at the airport by 6 p.m.

3) 전화로 탑승편 확인(C)

T : Tour Conductor	A : Airline's Staff

A : American Airlines, Mary speaking. May I help you?

T : I'd like to confirm my reservation.

A : Your name and flight number, please.

T : My name is Kim, and my flight number is AW 273.

A : You are leaving for London, Thursday at 1:30 p.m. Right?

T : Yes.

A : Hold on, please. OK, your reservation is confirmed.

T : Thank you a lot.

4) 전화로 탑승편 확인(D)

T : Tour Conductor	A : Airline's Staff

T : I'm calling to confirm a reservation on Flight 807 to Chicago tomorrow afternoon, the 25th. My name is Kim.

A : Just a moment, please. Mr. Kim... That reservation was made in New York?

T: Yes, it was.

A: All right. Thank you for calling to confirm. Is there anything else we can do for you?

T: Yes, please. Do you have a bus to the airport for that flight?

A: Yes, we do. It leaves from the central bus terminal three hours before flight time.

T: Thank you, and what is the baggage allowance for first class passengers within the international flight?

A: You're allowed 25kg, sir. And you may also carry on one small suitcase and put it under your seat.

T: I see. Thank you a lot.

A: Thank you for flying American Airlines.

5) 전화로 탑승편을 확인했는데 다른 단체의 이름으로 예약되어 있을 경우

T: Tour Conductor	**A:** Airline's Staff

T: Hello, Is this the American Airlines ticket counter?

A: Yes, it is. May I help you?

T : We need to confirm our booking on the flight to New York next Monday morning. We'll take American Airlines 210 to New York. We'd like to reconfirm reservations for our party of 30 people in all. Could you confirm it for me?

A : Of course, sir. Did you make reservations when you purchased the air tickets?

T : Yes, I did it in Seoul.

A : May I have your group's name, please?

T : It's Happy Tour.

A : Just a minute, let me check your reservation. Well, I am sorry but I don't see your name on the reservation list.

T : It could be listed under 'Kyungmin Culture Tourism Industry Research Center'. Could you check it carefully, please?

A : Hold on a minute, please. Oh, here it is. You're leaving for New York to take American Airlines 210 on next Monday. Right?

T : Yes.

A: Thirty seats are now confirmed. May I have your name and phone number, please?

T: I'm at Hanguk University, you can connect with me at 02-595-7228. My name is Mr. Kim.

A: Okay, sir. Your flight is scheduled to leave at 11 a.m.

T: When do we have to check in at the airport?

A: 9:00 a.m. at the least, sir.

T: Do you serve meals in the flight?

A: Yes, dinner and breakfast will be served.

T: Could I know the menu in advance?

A: I am sorry but I'm not sure of it right now. If you don't mind, I will call you later after I get an information.

T: That sound great. Thank you for your cooperation.

A: It's my pleasure, sir. I will call you later.

T: Thank you, bye.

(3) 항공편 예약 변경

T : Tour Conductor	**A :** Airline's Staff

A : Good morning. American Airlines. May I help you?

T : I'd like to change my reservation.

A : May I have your name and flight number?

T : My name is Kim, the flight number is AA 210 for New York on this Thursday.

A : Hold on, please. Yes, How would you like to change it?

T : I'd like to change it to a flight to Chicago leaving on this Saturday.

A: All right. We have flight AA 710 to Chicago on this Saturday at 8 p.m. Is it Okay?

T: Yes, I'll take it.

A: The change is done.

T: Thank you a lot.

A: It's my pleasure. Have a nice day.

(4) 항공편 예약 취소

T: Tour Conductor	A: Airline's Staff

A: American Airlines. May I help you.

T: I'd like to cancel my reservation for the flight to New York on this Sunday.

A: Could you tell me your name, sir?

T: My name is Kim.

A: Is there anything else, sir?

T: No. Thank you a lot.

(5) 항공 티켓 구매

T: Tour Conductor	A: Airline's Staff

A: Good morning. May I help you, sir?

T: I need to purchase my ticket.

A: Did you make a reservation, sir?

T : Sure. I already have a reservation.

A : All right What is your name and flight number?

T : My name is Kim and my flight number is AA210.

A : Yes. Mr. Kim, we have your reservation. You're leaving for New York on flight 210, economy class. It's $700 for a round-trip. Shall I book your return flight?

T : Yes. I want to reservation return flight ticket on August 31.

A : OK. How will you be paying?

T : Do you accept Master card?

A : Sure. May I have your credit card and ID card, please?

T : Here you are.

A : Hold on, please. I'll be right back. Thank you for waiting Mr. Kim. Would you sign here and put your phone number, please?

T : OK. Here it is.

A : Your ticket for New York, economy class, on Flight 210 leaving on August 25. Do you have any baggage?

T : Yes, I have one bag.

A: If you want, the porter can help you with checking in your baggage.

T: That sounds good.

A: Here is your ticket. You'll be departing from gate 21.

T: Thank you a lot.

(6) 항공사 카운터에서

1) 체크인(A)

T: Tour Conductor	**A:** Airline's Staff

A: Good morning. Can I help you?

T: Yes, I'd like to check in, please.

A: May I have your name, sir?

T: Kim from Happy Tour.

A: Yes, we have your reservation. May I see your ticket and passport, please?

T: Here your are.

A: Smoking or non-smoking, please?

T: Non-smoking, and I want five aisle seats, please.

A: Do you have any baggage?

T: Yes, I have thirty suitcase here.

A: If you want, we can check your baggage here.

T: Oh, good.

A: Would you put it on the scale, please?

T: Here you go.

A: Thank you. Your seat number is from 18H through 27A. Here are your passport, ticket, boarding pass and baggage claim tag. Have a nice flight.

T: Thank you. I'll.

2) 체크인(B)

T: Tour Conductor	**A:** Airline's Staff

T: Do I check in here for American Airlines flight 587 to Boston?

A : Do you already have your ticket?

T : Yes, here you are.

A : Thank you. Would you put your baggage on the scale, please?

T : Sure, I have two suitcases.

A : You are going to Boston on flight 587, first class, aren't you?

T : Right.

A : Would you like a window seat or an aisle seat?

T : I prefer an aisle seat.

A : Your seat number is 18C. Here are your ticket, passport and boarding pass.

T : What time is the flight leaving?

A : It will leave at 11 a.m.

T : Where do I go now?

A : Would you please go to Customs and Immigration?

T : Thank you so much.

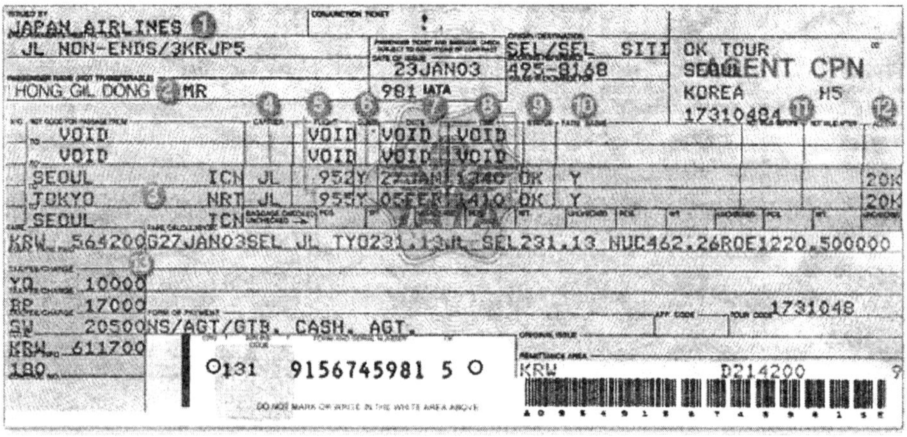

[그림 2] 항공권 견본

(7) 수화물

1) 중량 초과시(A)

T: Tour Conductor	A: Airline's Staff

T: Can I check in here for this flight?

A: Yes, you can. Your passport and ticket, please.

T: Here they are.

A: Can you put your baggage up this scale, sir?

T: All right.

A: Your baggage is overweighted.

T: How much is the extra charge?

A: The extra charge is 25 dollars.

T: OK. Here it is.

A: Here is your ticket and boarding pass. Have a good trip.

2) 중량 초과시(B)

T: Tour Conductor	**A:** Airline's Staff

A: Do you have any luggage?

T: Yes, I have three suitcases.

A: We allow only two pieces. You'll have to pay an extra charge.

T: How much is the extra charge?

A: 10 dollars per one kilogram.

T: Oh, can I carry these with me?

A : I'm sorry but they won't fit under your seat.

T : OK, when is the boarding time?

A : It's 2:30 p.m.

T : What's the gate number?

A : Gate number is 16.

(8) 보안 검색대

1) 보안 검색대를 지날 때(A)

T : Tour Conductor	**S :** Security

S : Put all carry on baggage on the conveyor, please. Step right this way, sir. please empty your pickets and go through, sir.

T : How about this digital camera?

S : You can give me it, sir. It doesn't have to go through the scanner.

T : OK.

S: Would I open your bag, sir?

T: Sure. There you go.

S: Would you mind turning off the CD player?

T: Oh, sorry.

S: That's ok. sir. Thank you for your cooperation.

2) 보안 검색대를 지날 때(B)

T: Tour Conductor	**S:** Security

(Beep)

S: Please step this way, sir. What do you have in this pocket?

T: Oh, I'm sorry, just some coin.

S: That's good. Thank you. Please put all carry-on baggage on the scale. Step right this carry-on. Would you mind opening your briefcase, sir?

T: No, not at all. There you go.

항공권 예약시에 자주 사용하는 질문 및 요구

1. I'd like to book a flight to New York.
2. How long does the flight take?
3. Your seat is reserved.
4. Which one would you like?
5. The fare is 250 dollars.
6. Do you have any spaces on that flight?
7. Please be present at gate 7 thirty minutes before departure time.
8. Which seat would you prefer, a window or an aisle seat?
9. May I see your ticket and passport?
10. Do you have any baggage to check?
11. I want to ticket for a flight to Chicago via Honolulu.
12. Would you like a round-trip or one-way ticket?
13. I want an one way, please.
14. Do you have a morning flight?
15. Your baggage is overweighted.

1. 뉴욕으로 가는 비행기를 예약하고 싶습니다.
2. 비행시간은 얼마나 됩니까?
3. 손님의 좌석이 예약되었습니다.
4. 어떤 것을 원하십니까?
5. 요금은 250달러입니다.
6. 그 비행기에 여분의 좌석이 있습니까?
7. 출발시간 30분 전까지 7번 출구로 오십시오.

8. 창가 쪽 자리를 드릴까요, 통로 쪽 자리를 드릴까요?
9. 표와 여권을 보여주시겠습니까?
10. 위탁 수하물을 가지고 계십니까?
11. 호놀룰루를 경유해서 시카고로 가는 비행 티켓을 원합니다.
12. 왕복권과 편도권 어느 것을 원하세요?
13. 편도권을 원합니다.
14. 오전 비행편이 있나요?
15. 중량 초과입니다.

2 기내에서의 각종 회화

(1) 기내에서 좌석을 찾을 때

1) 기내에서 좌석을 찾을 때 사용되는 회화(A)

T: Tour Conductor	A: Airline's Cabin Attendant

A: Good morning, sir. Welcome aboard. Would you show me your boarding pass?

T: Here it is.

A: Thank you. Your seat is 28C. It's in the back of the cabin, on your left, sir. May I help you with your bags?

T: No, thank you. Where can I put my bag?

A: You can put it underneath the seat in front of you or in the overhead compartment, sir. Please keep this heavy one is under your seat.

T: OK. I will.

2) 기내에서 좌석을 찾을 때 사용되는 회화(B)

T: Tour Conductor **A:** Airline's Cabin Attendant

T: Where's my seat?

A: Could I see the remainder of your boarding pass?

T: Here it is.

A: Thank you. Your seat is 26K. Go straight down 12 rows back.

T: Thank you. Are there any vacant seat?

A: Yes, but you have to wait until take-off?

T: OK. Can I recline this seat?

A: Not yet. You'd better wait until flying off.

3) 기내에서 좌석을 찾을 때 사용되는 회화(C)

T: Tour Conductor **A:** Airline's Cabin Attendant

T: Where can I put my bag?

A: You can put it underneath the seat in front of you or in the overhead compartment.

T: Where's the restroom?

A: At the back of the airplane, there are four bathrooms.

T: Are we ready to take off?

A: Yes, please sit your seat and fasten your seat belt.

T: I will.

4) 기내에서 좌석을 찾을 때 사용되는 회화(D)

T: Tour Conductor	**A:** Airline's Cabin Attendant

A: Boarding pass, please.

T: Here, it says seat 10G.

A: That will be on the left side, first section, on the aisle.

T: Thank you. Where can I place my hand carry?

A: There is a storage compartment just above your seat. Additionally, you'll find a pillow and blanket if you want to get a bit of rest before arriving.

T: I guess I'll need it. How long before we take off?

A: In about 10 minutes. If you want, we have a selection of magazines to help pass the time.

T: Thank you.

A: Just after take off, we'll be serving some drinks.

(2) 단체여행 때 기내에 들어가서 바로 사용하는 회화

T: Tour Conductor	**A:** Airline's Cabin Attendant

A: Good morning. Can I help you?

T: Good morning. We are all 30 people. Do you inform where our seat is? Four of us are non-smokers.

A: Would you show me your boarding pass?

T: Yes, here you are.

A: Your seat numbers are from 27-A through 30-H.
That will be on the left side, second section. Seats for non-smokers are 1-A, B. C. and D.

T : Thanks a lot.

A : Would you please tell your group to put their carry-on baggage under the seat, not on the overhead rack?

T : We have only a small bag. Where can we put our bags?

A : We can keep it in the storage bin on this aircraft. By the way, Are you the tour conductor of the Happy Tour group? My name is Enya.

T : Glad to meet you Miss Enya. I'm the tour conductor and my name is Kim.

A : Where's your destination?

T : New York. May I look at your menu to help our group to take orders for meals?

A : That's very kind of you, Mr. Kim.

T : What kind of drinks do you have?

A : We serve alcoholic and non-alcoholic beverages.

T : Do you have any caffeine-free coffee?

A : Sorry, We have no caffeine-free coffee in our pantry.

T: OK. When do you serve dinner on this flight?

A: We will serve it at five.

T: OK. Could you serve my group something to read?

A: Of course, sir.

T: Thank you. And we need more blankets. Do you have any extra ones?

A: Yes, We have some in the overhead rack.

T: OK. Are you showing any special movie today?

A: Yes, We have one.

T: What's that?

A: It's 'Troy'.

T: That sounds good. Thank you.

A: You're welcome, sir. Have a good time.

(3) 좌석 변경시

1) 좌석을 변경하고 싶을 때(A)

T: Tour Conductor **A:** Airline's Cabin Attendant

T: Excuse me, Miss. I'd like to change a seat if possible.

A: Is there a problem with this seat, sir?

T: One of our members has acrophobia, and the sight out of window scares her.

A: Let me see what can I do. After everyone has boarded, I'll come back and let you know, sir.

T: Thank you a lot.

A: (after a while) Thank you for waiting, sir. We have some empty seats in the end line. Would that be all right?

T: Sure, that will be just right.

A: Please come this way. Here you are.

T: Thank you very much.

A: You're welcome. Have a nice trip, sir.

2) 좌석을 변경하고 싶을 때(B)

T: Tour Conductor　　　**A:** Airline's Cabin Attendant

T: Can I change my seat? It would be really nice of you if you could do that.

A: Is there a problem with this seat, sir?

T: No, I hate smoking so I'd like to move to the non-smoking section.

A: Let me see what can I do. Yes, we have lots of vacant seats in the non-smoking section. Please come this way, sir.

T: Thank you so much.

(4) 이륙할 때

T: Tour Conductor　　　**A:** Airline's Cabin Attendant

A: Sir, Fasten your seat belt and adjust your seat to the upright position, please.

T: I'm afraid I don't know how to do it.

A: Pull this belt like this and fasten this.

T: Thanks. Oh, something is wrong with the seat. I can't recline it.

A: Press this, and it goes this way. Is it OK?

T: Oh, I see, and I feel like throwing up. Would you give me some medicine for airsickness and airsick bag?

A: Just a minute, sir. I'll bring you some medicine in a moment. Traveling by airplane is very comfortable these days. Today planes have hardly any vibration unless the weather is exceptionally bad.

T: OK.

(5) 음료 서비스

1) 음료 서비스를 받을 때(A)

T: Tour Conductor	**A:** Airline's Cabin Attendant

T: Excuse me. Our members want to drink something. Do you give us Something to drink?

A: What would you like to drink, sir?

T: Do you have a soft drink?

A: Sure. We have seven-up, coke, orange juice, tomato juice, pineapple juice and mango juice. Which beverage do you want?

T: We want five coke with plenty of ice, twelve mango juice, and thirteen seven-up.

A: OK. Just a second, sir. I'll be right back with them.

2) 음료 서비스를 받을 때(B)

T: Tour Conductor	**A:** Airline's Cabin Attendant

T: Excuse me. Do you have something to drink?

A: What would you like to drink?

T: Do you have a Jin and Tonic?

A: Sure. Just a minutes, sir. I'll be right back with it.

3) 음료 서비스를 받을 때(C)

T: Tour Conductor	**A**: Airline's Cabin Attendant

A: Would you care for a drink?

T: Yes, what do you have?

A: We have orange juice, tomato juice, tea, coffee and coke.

T: Tea with a slice of lemon, please.

A: Here you are, sir.

T: Thank you. How much is it?

A: There is no charge for tea, coffee and coke.

(6) 식사 서비스

1) 식사 서비스를 받을 때(A)

T: Tour Conductor	**A**: Airline's Cabin Attendant

A: Please return your seat to the upright position. We'll be serving meals, soon. Would you pull out your table, sir?

T: Sure

A: Which would you like, chicken or beef?

T: How about fish? One of our members is a vegetarian.

A: I'm sorry but we don't have fish. But if you want, We can serve seafood spaghetti.

T: OK. I'll do it, and nine chicken and twenty beef, please.

A: Would you like to drink some wine? We have white wine and red wine.

T: Please five white wine and fifteen red wine. Some of our members can't drink. So could you give them soft drink?

A: Of course, Here you go. Enjoy your meal.

T: Thank you.

2) 식사 서비스를 받을 때(B)

T: Tour Conductor	**A:** Airline's Cabin Attendant

A: Would you care for lunch?

T: Yes, please.

A: We have three selections, the traditional American style beef steak, a Korean style bulgogi-backban and a Chinese style jajang-myun. What will you want?

T: I'll take the Chinese style lunch.

A: Would you like to drink some wine or another cocktail? We have white wine and red wine.

T: White wine, please.

A: Here you go, anything else?

T: No, thank you. That's enough.

A: Enjoy your meal.

3) 식사 서비스를 받을 때(C)

T: Tour Conductor	**A:** Airline's Cabin Attendant

A: How can I help you, sir?

T: May I ask you a question?

A: Of course.

T: When do you serve dinner on this flight? I'm starving.

A: We will serve it at 6.

T: It's 5p.m. So I have to wait one hour from now.

A: No, you should wait two hours. We use Eastern Time.

T: Oh, I see.

A: I'll serve you something to drink instead.

T: Thank you.

(7) 기내 서비스

1) 담요와 기내 영화 서비스(A)

T: Tour Conductor	**A:** Airline's Cabin Attendant

T: Miss! May I have a blanket, please?

A: Sure. Here they are.

T: Thank you. How can I turn off this light?

A: Just push this button here. You can take the arm off. Then you can have a nice rest.

T: OK. Thanks a lot. Are you showing a special movie?

A: We have an animation today. The name of the movie is "Shrek"

T: Oh, I like it.

A: I'll bring you an earphone. You can enjoy stereo music, too.

T: Good. What channel is the movie on?

A: In English on channel 2 and in Korean on 1.

2) 담요와 기내 영화 서비스(B)

T: Tour Conductor **A:** Airline's Cabin Attendant

T: I'd like to take a map. May I have a blanket and a pillow, please?

A: Wait a moment, please. Here they are.

T: Thank you. And May I have an earphone?

A: Do you want to see a movie?

T: No, I'd like to listen to music.

A: OK, I'll bring you an earphone. You can enjoy stereo music.

T: What channel is the music?

A: 3 through 14. 3 through 6 are Korean music, 7 through 11 are American music, 12 is Japanese music, 13 is Chinese music, and 14 is European music.

T: Thank you very much.

3) 담요와 기내 영화 서비스(C)

T: Tour Conductor　　**A:** Airline's Cabin Attendant

T: Good evening, We are tour group of 30.

A: Oh, are you a tour conductor?

T: Yes, May I have some more blankets, if you have any extra ones?

A: Of course. We have some in the overhead rack.

T: Thank you.

(after a while)

T: Excuse me. One of my members feels like throwing up. Do you have any medicine to aid digestion?

A: Yes, I'll bring you some medicine.

T: Thank you, and I think I need a paper bag.

A: Here you are.

(after a while) Does he feel better?

T: Yes, he feels much better.

(8) 도착시간 문의

T: Tour Conductor	**A:** Airline's Cabin Attendant

T: Excuse me. What time are we arriving at New York?

A: Let me see. We are arriving at 11 a.m, local time.

T: I see. What's the flying time from Seoul to New York?

A: It's about eleven hours.

T: And what's the time difference between Seoul and New York?

A: It's thirteen hours. Seoul is thirteen hours ahead.

T: Are we losing or gaining a day on the way to America?

A: We are gaining a day. It means we're arriving on the same day.

T: Oh, I see.

(9) 입국 신고서 및 세관 신고서 기재

T: Tour Conductor　　**A:** Airline's Cabin Attendant

A: Fill out the landing card, please.

T: Miss! Can you help me?

A: Yes. What can I help you, sir?

T: I've completed my customs declaration form. Is it all right?

A: If you have valuables and U.S dollars amounting more than 10,000 dollars, you should declare them.

T: OK.

A: And you have to write your passport number and visa number here, sir.

T: Thank for your help. Is it all right now?

A: Yes, sir.

(10) 착륙할 때

T: Tour Conductor	A: Airline's Cabin Attendant

A: Excuse me, sir. Please fasten your seat belt. We're going to land now.

T: OK.

A: Please remain in your seat until the aircraft comes to a complete stop.

T: We're in Chicago at last. It was a smooth landing, wasn't it?

A: Yes, sure it was. I hope you enjoyed your flight.

T: Yes, indeed. Thanks for a good service.

A: It's my pleasure. It's our duty. What's your final destination?

T: New York. I have to get off at Kennedy Airport.

A: Well, I have to say good bye now. Hope to see you again.

T: So do I. Thank you.

기내에서의 여흥거리

A wide selection of Korean and International publications is available for your enjoyment. You may keep this complimentary copy of Morning Calm, but kindly return all other reading materials after you have finished with them for the benefit of fellow passengers. To add your enjoyment, an international selection of music is available on eight different channels, from channel 3 to 10, located on the dial on your armrest. We also offer a selection of popular films in our inflight movie program. You may listen to the movie in English on channel 2 or in Korean on 1.

한국 출판물과 국제 출판물의 폭넓은 선택은 여러분에게 흥미를 제공할 것입니다. 여러분은 모닝 캄을 무료로 보실 수 있으며, 다 보신 후에는 다른 승객들을 위하여 제자리에 놓아두시길 바랍니다. 여러분의 흥미를 더하기 위하여 팔걸이에 위치한 채널은 3에서 10까지 8개의 여러 나라의 음악을 제공하고 있습니다. 또한 기내에서 유명한 영화를 상영하고 있습니다. 2번 채널로는 영어로 영화를 즐기실 수 있으며, 1번 채널은 한국어로 즐기실 수 있습니다.

기내에서의 각종 문의사항에 대한 회화

T: Tour Conductor **A:** Airline's Cabin Attendant

1. T: Can I lean this seat back?

   A: Not yet. You have to wait until the flight takes off.

   T: 의자에 기대도 됩니까?

   A: 아직은 안 됩니다. 비행기가 이륙할 때까지 기다리셔야 합니다.

2. T: Can I have some water?

   A: Yes. When everyone has boarded, I will get it for you, sir.

   T: 물 좀 주시겠습니까?

   A: 예. 모든 손님이 다 탑승하신 후에 가져다 드리겠습니다.

3. T: May I take off my seat belt?

   A: No. You have to wait until the light goes off.

   T: 안전벨트를 풀어도 됩니까?

   A: 안 됩니다. 불이 꺼질 때까지 기다려주십시오.

4. T: Where is the restroom?

   A: At the back of the airplane, there are three bathrooms.

   T: 화장실은 어디에 있습니까?

   A: 비행기 뒤쪽에 3개의 화장실이 있습니다.

5. T: Are we ready to take off?

   A: Yes. Please bring your seat back forward and fasten your seat belt.

   T: 이륙할 준비가 되었습니까?

   A: 예. 의자를 앞으로 당겨주시고, 벨트를 매주십시오.

6. T: How long before we take off?

   A: In about 20 minutes.

   T: Still seems like a long time.

   A: If you like, we have a selection of magazines to help pass the time.

   T: Thank you.

   A: Just after take off, we'll be serving refreshments.

   T: 이륙은 언제 하나요?

   A: 20분 안에 이륙할 예정입니다.

   T: 길게 느껴지네요.

   A: 원하신다면 시간을 보내실 수 있도록 잡지를 드릴까요?

   T: 감사합니다.

   A: 이륙하면 곧 간단한 음식물을 제공해드릴 것입니다.

기내에서 자주 사용하는 질문 및 요구

1. Where are we flying now? Are we on schedule?
2. What is the local time in New York?
3. I want to take some pictures through the window. Does it bother you?
4. Would you show me some magazines or newspapers?

5. Which would you like for dinner, beef or chicken?
6. Give me some more cocktail, please.
7. Something is wrong with the seat. I can't recline it. Can you check it?
8. Could you turn the reading-light a little aslant? I'd like to sleep.
9. Please show me how to fill out this form.
10. I have trouble breathing, and I feel like throwing up. Can you give him (her) some pill for airsickness?
11. How long before we land in New York?
12. Can I move to the non-smoking section. I hate smoking.
13. Would you mind trading seats with me?
14. How long will it take from New York to Honolulu?

1. 지금 어디쯤 비행하고 있습니까? 예정대로입니까?
2. 뉴욕 현지시간을 가르쳐 주시겠습니까?
3. 창 쪽에서 사진을 찍고 싶은데 괜찮겠습니까?
4. 잡지나 신문을 보여 주시겠습니까?
5. 저녁은 소고기나 닭고기 중에서 어느 쪽으로 하시겠습니까?
6. 칵테일 좀더 주세요.
7. 좌석이 고장입니다. 뒤로 젖힐 수가 없습니다. 봐주시겠어요?
8. 독서 램프를 조절해도 될까요. 자고 싶어요
9. 이 세관 신고서를 기재하는 방법을 알려주십시오.
10. 호흡이 곤란하고 토하고 싶습니다. 멀미약 있습니까?
11. 뉴욕에 도착하려면 얼마나 있어야 하죠?
12. 금연구역으로 옮길 수 있겠습니까? 담배를 싫어하거든요.
13. 저와 자석을 바꾸지 않으시겠습니까?
14. 뉴욕에서 호놀룰루까지 얼마나 걸립니까?

기 내 방 송

비행기가 이륙하기 전, 비상시 구명조끼, 산소 마스크 사용법, 출발 지연, 목적지 도착 후의 안내방송 등이 나온다.

• 항공기내 방송 - 출발 직전

Good morning, ladies and gentlemen. This is captain Steve speaking. I would like to welcome you aboard American Airlines. This flight 210 is now leaving for New York via Anchorage. Having departed Incheon International Airport on time, we are now cruising at 38,000 feet, with a ground speed of 780 miles an hour. Our flight time after take off will be 10 hour and 30 minutes and we should arrive in New York at 11 a.m., local time. The weather en route is forecast to be generally fair with occasional turbulence. Please, put your seat to the upright position, fasten your seat belt, and refrain from smoking until 'No smoking' sign is turned off. I wish you a pleasant flight. Thank you.

신사 숙녀 여러분 안녕하십니까? 저는 여러분을 뉴욕까지 모시고 갈 기장 스티브입니다. 오늘도 아메리칸 에어라인을 이용해주셔서 감사합니다. 이 비행기 210편은 앵커리지를 경유하여 뉴욕에 도착할 예정입니다. 현재 이 항공기는 인천 국제공항을 이륙하여 고도 38,000피트 시속 780마일로 비행중에 있습니다. 뉴욕까지의 비행시간은 이륙으로부터 10시간 30분이 소요되어 현지시간 오전 11시에 도착할 예정입니다. 오늘 항공상의 날씨는 대체로 양호한 것으로 예보되었으나 가끔 기체 동요가 예상됩니다. 좌석을 바로 해주시고 안전벨트를 착용하시고, 담배는 금연등에 불이 꺼질 때까지 삼가주시기 바랍니다. 여러분의 즐거운 여행이 되시길 바랍니다. 감사합니다.

• 항공기내 방송 - 기체가 흔들릴 때

Ladies and gentlemen, This is your captain speaking. We expect to have some turbulence in a few minutes. So please return to your seat and fasten the seat belt. We will be out of this turbulent area in about 20 minutes. Thank you.

신사 숙녀 여러분, 저는 기장입니다. 잠시 후 기류 관계로 인하여 기체가 다소 흔들릴 것으로 예상됩니다. 좌석으로 돌아가셔서 좌석 벨트를 매어주시기 바랍니다. 약 20분 후에는 다시 잠잠해질 것으로 예상됩니다. 감사합니다.

• 항공기내 방송 - 비상상태일 때

Attention, please. Please follow these instructions carefully. Please put any sharp objects you may have, such as eyeglasses, fountain pens and so on into the seat pocket in front of you. Gentlemen, loosen your neckties. Ladies, please remove your high heeled shoes. Your life vest is located under your seat. Please, put your vest on soon now. To inflate your vest, pull the two tabs straight down. Do not do this until you are out of the cabin.

안내방송입니다. 다음 지시를 유의하여 따라주시기를 바랍니다. 여러분께서 소지하고 계시는 안경이나 만년필 등 뾰족한 물체는 모두 꺼내셔서 앞좌석 호주머니에 집어넣으십시오. 그리고 신사분들께서는 넥타이를 푸시고, 숙녀분들께서는 굽이 높은 신발은 벗으십시오. 그리고 여러분들의 구명조끼는 여러분 좌석 밑에 있습니다. 지금 곧 구명조끼를 입으시고, 구명조끼에 공기가 팽팽히 들어가도록 조끼 옆에 달린 두 끈을 밑으로 당기십시오. 그러나 비행기 밖으로 나가기 전에는 그렇게 하시면 안 됩니다.

• 항공기내 방송 - 경유지 공항에서 1

May I have your attention, please? We have just landed at Anchorage International Airport. Passengers continuing on to LosAngels, please remain on board. This flight 015 will stay on the ground for 40 minutes. Thank you.

신사 숙녀 여러분. 안내방송에 귀를 기울여주십시오. 우리는 방금 앵커리지 국제공항에 도착하였습니다. LA로 가시는 승객께서는 자리에 남아 계십시오. 저희 015편은 40분간 지상에 머무를 예정입니다. 감사합니다.

• 항공기내 방송 - 경유지 공항에서 2

Ladies and gentlemen. May I have your attention, please? We have just landed at Los Angeles International Airport. Transit passengers continuing on to New York, please receive your transit card from the American Airlines agent when you deplane and wait in the terminal building until your flight is called.

신사 숙녀 여러분. 안내말씀 드리겠습니다. 우리는 방금 로스엔젤레스 국제공항에 도착했습니다. 뉴욕으로 계속 가실 승객분들께서는 내리실 때 저희 아메리칸 에어라인 직원이 드린 환승 카드를 받으신 후 대합실에서 여러분이 탑승하실 다음 비행기에 대한 안내방송이 있을 때까지 대기하여주시기 바랍니다.

• 항공기내 방송 - 도착 전

Ladies and gentlemen, we are no flying at an altitude of 25,000 feet and at a ground speed of 700 miles per hours. We expect to arrive in New York in about two hours. The weather in New York is foggy and the temperature is 28 degrees celsius or 82 degrees Fahrenheit.

신사 숙녀 여러분, 우리는 지금 25,000피트의 고도를 시속 700마일의 속도로 날고 있습니다. 우리는 약 2시간 후에 뉴욕에 도착할 예정입니다. 현재 뉴욕의 날씨는 안개가 끼어 있으며, 기온은 섭씨 28도, 화씨 82도입니다.

• 기장의 일반적인 아나운스

1. We expect to land in New York in local time 10 hours and 30 minutes.
2. The time difference between Seoul and New York is 17 hours.
3. If you'd like to set your watch, it is now 30minutes after five Monday morning New York time.
4. After we land in Kennedy Airport, first of all, We should go through Quarantine and Immigration.
5. Please have your vaccination card and passport with you.
6. There is customs inspection here.
7. After completing government procedures, please proceed to the airport transit room where beverages will be served.
8. The air craft will be on the ground for about three hour.
9. In a few minutes, we'll be landing at Kennedy Airport.
10. At this time, would you please bring your seat to an up right position and fasten your seat belt for landing?
11. We'd like to remind you to check the overhead racks, underneath the seats and seat pockets so that you don't forget your personal effects when you leave the aircraft
12. Please remain seated until the aircraft has come to a complete stop.
13. After the captain has turned on the 'No-Smoking' sign, would you please extinguish all your cigarettes?

14. It has been a pleasure to have you aboard today. We hope you have enjoyed your flight and that we may serve you again soon.

1. 뉴욕까지의 소요시간은 약 10시간 30분 예정하고 있습니다.
2. 서울과 뉴욕의 시차는 17시간입니다.
3. 시계를 현지시간으로 맞추고 싶은 손님께서는 지금 뉴욕 시간으로 금요일 오전 5시 30분입니다.
4. 케네디 공항에 도착하면 우선 검역과 입국심사를 합니다.
5. 예방접종 증명서와 여권은 반드시 갖고 계십시오.
6. 이쪽은 세관검사입니다.
7. 수속이 끝나면 공항 특별대합실 쪽으로 가주세요. 음료수가 준비되어 있습니다.
8. 이 비행기의 대기시간은 약 3시간 예정입니다.
9. 이 비행기는 곧 케네디 공항에 착륙하겠습니다.
10. 의자 위치를 원래의 위치로 해주시고 안전띠를 매주세요.
11. 보관함, 좌석 밑, 시트포켓 등 잊으신 물건이 없도록 주위 물건을 잘 확인해주세요.
12. 완전히 정지할 때까지 앉은 채 기다려주세요.
13. 기장이 금연의 사인을 내면 담뱃불을 꺼주세요.
14. 탑승해주신 여러분 감사합니다. 다시 기내에서 만날 수 있기를 승무원 일동은 바랍니다.

대한민국 입국신고서 /ARRIVAL CARD ①
REPUBLIC OF KOREA 入國申告書 IMMIGRATION SERVICE

한글성명 / Surname / 姓	漢字姓名
Given Names / 名	
생년월일 Date of Birth / 生年月日 Year 年 Month 月 Day 日 / 주민등록 뒷번호	남/MALE/ 男 M / 여/FEMALE/ 女 F
국적 Nationality 國籍	여권번호 /Passport No./旅券番號
한국내 주소 / Address in Korea / 韓國內 住所 (Tel:)	
직업 직장명 Occupation /職業	여행목적/Purpose of visit 旅行目的
출발지(국가/도시) / 出發地 Last City / Port of Boarding	입국편명 · 선명 / 入國便名 · 船名 Flight No. / Vessel on Arrival PR
공용란 公用欄 Official Use Only PRA04285234E	서명 / Signature / 署名

TYPE OR PRINT BOTH SIDES 양쪽 모두 기재 兩側記載

대한민국 출국신고서 /DEPARTURE CARD ②
REPUBLIC OF KOREA 出國申告書 IMMIGRATION SERVICE
REFER TO THE BACK HOW TO FILL UP

한글성명 / Surname / 姓	漢字姓名
Given Names / 名	
생년월일 Date of Birth / 生年月日 Year 年 Month 月 Day 日 / 주민등록 뒷번호	남/MALE/ 男 M / 여/FEMALE/ 女 F
국적 Nationality 國籍	여권번호 /Passport No./旅券番號
한국내 주소 / Address in Korea / 韓國內 住所 (Tel:)	
직업 직장명 /Occupation/職業	여행목적 Purpose of visit 旅行目的
목적지(국가/도시) / 目的地 Next City / Port of Landing	출국편명 · 선명 / 出國便名 · 船名 Flight No. / Vessel on Departure PR
공용란 公用欄 Official Use Only PRA04285234D	서명 / Signature / 署名

[그림 3] 대한민국 출 · 입국 신고서

3 검역과 통관수속

(1) 검역에서의 회화

O : Officer	T : Tour Conductor

O : Could you show me your health card.

T : OK, here you are.

O : Are you vaccinated against SARS?

T : No, no SARS shot was made. We come from Korea.

O : Oh, I see. All right. Now Proceed to the passport check.

(2) 입국수속 회화

T : Tour Conductor	O : Officer

T : Good morning.

O : Good morning. May I see your passport, please?

T : Here you go.

C : Where are you from?

T : I'm from Korea.

C : Are you the tour conductor of this Korean group?

T : Yes, I am.

C : How many people are there in your party?

T : Thirty, including me.

C : What's the purpose of your visit? on a business trip or on a pleasure trip?

T : On pleasure.

C : How long are you going to stay in America?

T : We are staying here about one month.

C : Where are you going to stay?

T: In New York we stay at the Hilton Hotel.

C: Where are you going to tour?

T: After 10days in New York, we are visiting Boston, Chicago, and Las Vegas.

O: How nice. Here's your passport.

T: Thanks.

O: Welcome to the United States. Enjoy your trip.

T: Thank you. we will.

(3) 세관심사 회화

O : Officer	T : Tour Conductor

O : Good morning, sir. Do you have anything to declare?

T : No. Nothing to declare. We are a party of 30. I'm the tour conductor. We have 30 bags in all.

O : Don't you have any liquor, cigarettes, pearls and the like?

T : Each of us has less than two bottles of whisky, 100 cigarettes, but has not any pearls, precious metals or jewels.

O : Do you have any plant or animal?

T : No. I don't.

C: That's OK. Open your baggage, please. What is this?

T: This is powder of roast grain, a kind of food for me.

C: What's that box?

T: That is my medicine for heart.

C: What's that wrapped in the paper?

T: It's a dried squid.

C: And this?

T: These are some instant noodle.

C: Well, that's all right. Thank you for your cooperation.

T: It's my pleasure, sir.

C: Have a nice trip.

T: Thanks a lot. Good-bye.

(4) 짐 분실시

T: Tour Conductor	**A:** Airline Representative

T: Excuse me. My baggage hasn't arrived yet.

A: Take it easy, sir. Which flight?

T: Um, American Airlines from Seoul.

A: The flight number AA 210?

T: Yes. Everyone else's luggage come off the baggage claim, and now it's stopped. But mine never arrived.

A: Oh, I'm sorry. Did it have your name and address on it?

T: Of course. I had my name, address, zip code and cell-phone number on it.

A: We'll try to find it for you, sir. Can you fill out this form? And description for the bag, flight number, value of contents, etc.

T: OK.

A: Do you have an itemized list of the contents?

T: No. Why?

A: Your insurance company might ask for an itemized list. You'd better write one.

T: OK. I'm so nervous. One of my friends lost his suitcase a month ago and he hasn't found it yet.

A: Don't worry, and take it easy. Most of the lost baggage turn up someplace.

T: I hope so.

A: If it doesn't turn up within twelve hours, your insurance will pay for the things you need right now-a clean shirt, socks, underwear-that kind of thing.

T: OK.

통관수속시 사용하는 회화

1. What's the purpose of your visit?
2. For sightseeing/On business/I'm a tourist.
3. How many people in your party?
4. How long will you be in the United States?
5. Which hotel will you stay?
6. Anything to declare?
7. They are all my personal effects.
8. Do you have your customs declaration form?
9. What kind of items do I have to declare?
10. Where is the baggage claim area?

1. 방문 목적이 무엇입니까?
2. 관광차/사업차/나는 관광객입니다.
3. 일원이 몇 명입니까?
4. 미국에서는 얼마동안 체류할 예정입니까?
5. 어느 호텔에서 투숙하실 겁니까?
6. 신고하실 것은 없으십니까?
7. 그것은 모두 다 나의 개인용품입니다.
8. 입국 신고서는 다 작성하셨습니까?
9. 어떤 물품을 신고해야 합니까?
10. 수하물 찾는 곳은 어디에 있습니까?

4 포터와의 회화

(1) 환승버스에 탈 때 수화물 관리와 포터와의 대화

T: Tour Conductor **P**: Porter

T: Good morning. Could you take these bags and put them on the Happy Tour's bus?

P: Of course. How many bags do you have?

T: Thirty in all. They are the ones all with Happy Tour's white tags for identification.

P: Good. May I have your claim tags?

T: Here you are. How many pieces of baggage do you count?

P: Exactly.

T: Please take care of these baggages for a minute. I'll check the bus and be right back.

American Customs

Birthday spankings

The mock spanking administered to a birthday boy or girl recalls a rite that has long been an integral feature of many initiation ceremonies. The "public" spanking highlights the specialness of the child and invites the child back into the fold by offering him or her luck(one to grow on) and congratulations.

A: I can hardly wait. My birthday is coming up in two more days.

B: (Jokingly) Will you still be getting your little birthday spanking to wish you lock and an extra one to grow on?

A: Get serious! Sure, Mom and Dad always pretended to "pat" my behind and tell me that I needed an extra one to grow on when I was growing up. But I'm, already six feet, two inches tall. Does it, look like I need to grow any more?

American Superstitions

Fingernail clippings must not be left for others to find

An old American belief says that fingernails can by used to cost spells on their owner. The clippings must never be left around for the evil spirits to find. To be safe they should be burned or buried.

A: I can't believe all the things that have gone wrong since I broke up with my girlfriend. I lost my car keys, my TV was stolen, and I have a terrible cold.

B : Maybe she put a spell on you to get even.

A : How could she do that?

B : Well, you know how she hated to find your fingernail clippings on the floor. Maybe she used them to call out the evil spirits.

* 자료 : 《101 American Customs》 《101 American Superstitions》에서 발췌

Chapter 2

공항에서 호텔까지

미팅 서비스

현지 여행사 직원이 공항에 나오기로 되어 있다면 공항에서 현지 여행업자의 미팅 스태프와 만나 호텔까지 버스의 확인 등에 관해 미팅한다. 미팅 스태프는 현지 여행업자가 만들어준 인환증을 일정표와 같이 지참하고 있다. 공항에서 인환증을 받을 수 없으면 가능한 한 빨리 입수하고, 내용이 계약과 맞는지 재확인하고 현지 호텔, 버스회사, 주요관광지의 장소와 전화번호, 책임자 등이 기입되어 있는가를 체크한다.

환승버스의 의논

현지 여행사 직원이 공항에 나오지 않고 버스 운전사만 나오는 경우가 있다.

자신의 버스도 운전사도 발견되지 않을 때에는 가까이 있는 다른 버스 운전사 또는 포터에게 물으면 상황을 알 수 있는 경우가 많다. 상황을 전혀 모르는 경우에는 일단 대기하고 있는 관광버스 중 호텔까지 시간적으로 왕복할 수 있는 차량이 있는지를 조사하고, 그래도 안 되면 택시에 탑승하여 일단 예정 호텔까지 유도해야 한다. 이때에는 맨 처음 차에 현지 언어 또는 영어가 통하는 고객을 태워 호텔에 도착한 후 환전을 하여 요금을 지불한 다음 차례로 다음의 차량이 도착하는 것을 기다려 요금을 계산해주도록 한다.

렌터카, 리무진버스 등의 이용

리무진은 소정의 터미널까지 가지 않으니까 거기에서 호텔까지는 택시를 사용하기로 한다. 렌터카를 빌릴 때는 호텔과 동일하다.

버스에서의 안내

공항과 호텔간의 이동중인 버스 속에서는 여행객 전원의 얼굴을 볼 수 있고 마이크를 사용하므로 정보를 전달하는 데 절호의 기회이다. 그러나 한국에서 장시간의 항공여행을 거쳐 도착한 직후에는 모두 피곤해 있고, 조는 사람이 많으므로 이야기는 최소한 필요한 만큼만 하기로 한다.

1 미팅 서비스와 짐의 의논

(1) 공항에 도착하였을 때

1) 현지 여행사와 미팅 스태프와의 대화(A)

T : Tour Conductor R : Representative of Local Travel Agent

R : Excuse me, but aren't you Mr. Kim from the Happy Tour?

T : Yes, I'm. Are you Mr. Lee from the Global Travel Agency.

R : Yes. Nice to meet you, Mr. Kim. Welcome to New York.

T : Nice to meet you, too.

R : How was your flight?

T : It was great trip. Thank you anyway for coming out here to meet our group.

R : It's my pleasure. You came by American Airline, didn't you?

T : Yes. The service was very good.

R : Good. I'm told you have 30 people. Are they all here?

T : Yes. There are 30 people including me in my group.

R : I see. Is this all the baggage you have? Please check again to see if you've got everything.

T : Yes. That's all. We have 30 bags with Happy Tour' white tags.

R : Oh, I see. Our driver will handle your baggage. Come this way, please.

T : Thank you. Mr. Lee.

R : Where are you going to stay?

T : Hilton Hotel.

R : That's one of the best hotels in New York. I will give you a ride to your hotel.

T : Oh, Thank you. Can I have our voucher?

R : Yes. But I don't have it now. I'll give you it on the bus.

T : OK, Thank you.

2) 현지 여행사와 미팅 스태프와의 대화(B)

T: Tour Conductor **R**: Representative of Local Travel Agent

T: Are you from American Travel?

R: Yes, You're Kim! I'm Daniel. How are you! Welcome to Washington, D.C.

T: Very well. How are you! Nice to meet you. Please take these suitcases and put them on the bus. And we are 31, include me.

R: OK. Are you all on board?

T: Yes, now, can I have our voucher?

R: Certainly, here is your voucher. And here are 31 copies of your tour itinerary.

T: Good, thank you.

2 환승버스의 의논

(1) 현지 여행사의 미팅 스태프와 환승할 버스와의 미팅

T : Tour Conductor **R :** Representative of Local Travel Agent

T : Where is the bus we take?

R : Our bus is parked at the behind of this airport. It's a small walk from here. I'll show you where the bus is.

T : Oh, I see. Now shall we take the bus?

R : Yes. Are you all on board?

T : Ten of our members is now in the restroom. Hold the bus for a minute, please.

R : OK.

T : Are all of the baggages?

R : 30 pieces all together. Here are your vouchers and 30 copies of your tour itinerary.

T : Thank you. Mr. Kim.

R: You'll see 30 coupons in a batch. Will you please check it?

T: Everything is exactly. No problem.

R: If you have any changes, fill out our reverse side of the coupon in detail and endorse it, please.

T: OK. I will. We are all here now. Shall we go now?

3 리무진버스, 렌터카 등의 이용방법

(1) 수배한 버스가 공항에 안 왔을 경우

T: Tour Conductor **P:** Porter **B:** Bus Lines Staff

P: Where is your bus?

T: The bus can be here. It's Global Travel's bus. Isn't that blue one ours?

P: No. It's for another party.

T: I'll contact the bus line to see what happened. Where can I find a public telephone?

P: Go straight ahead this way. Have you got coin? You need a coin for city call.

T: I got it. (Speaking on the phone) Hello, is this Global Travel? Can I speak to the dispatcher?

B: Dispatcher Jee-Na speaking. May I help you?

T: This is the tour conductor of Happy Tour in Korea.

P: We are all here now at the airport waiting for your bus. But I can't find the bus.

B: Please go speaking.

T: I tried to find your bus, but couldn't. What's happening?

B: I didn't know you were coming in on this early flight. You are expected to arrive by American Airline flight 210 at 2 p.m.

T: It couldn't be, we are all here anyway there must wrong on your side.

B: Now, I'll call the bus terminal to send a bus to the

airport right now. Can you wait for an hour?

T : We can't wait so long. All of our members are very upset. Can we cancel your bus and take a limousine bus to Hotel?

B : If you want to cancel the bus, I must agree to cancel the arrangement.

T : Call Hilton Hotel at 1 o'clock this afternoon. My name is Kim. Let us talk about this discrepancy at that time in detail.

B : Very well, I'll call you at 1 again. Thank you for calling.

(2) 리무진버스의 이용

T : Tour Conductor　　　**L :** Limousines Driver

T : Does this limousine bus stop at the Hilton Hotel?

L : Yes, it does. Are you traveling alone?

T : No. I am traveling in a group of 30 people with baggages.

L : Bring your bags right here, so that I may put them on the bus.

T : How much is the fare?

L : It's 5 dollars per person to the Hotel. You pay me now.

T : Here's 150 dollars for 30 people. Can I get a receipt of that amount?

L : I'll work it out as soon as we arrive at the Hotel and give it to you there.

T : OK. How long does it take to the Hilton Hotel?

L : It takes one hour. (after 1 hour) We are now approaching Hilton Hotel. Have a good time.

T : Thanks a lot. We will.

(3) 렌터카 이용시

1) 렌터카 직원과의 대화(A)

T : Traveler	**R :** Rent-a-Car Office's Staff

R : Good morning. May l help you?

T : Good morning. I'd like to rent a car.

R : How long do you want to rent a car?

T : For about 7 days.

R : OK. Which model would you like?

T : May I have your brochure?

R : Here you are.

T : (Pause) I'll take this one.

R : All right. May I see your driver's license and credit card?

T : Here you are. It's international driver's license.

R : Do you have any identification cards besides this license?

T : I have my passport there.

R : Fine.

T : How much is the rate?

R : The national average daily rate is $45 a day and 20 cents per mile.

T : What items are included in the rate?

R : It includes gas, oil and insurance, regardless of how many rides.

T : Can I leave the car at your Kennedy Airport office?

R : Yes, you can. How about the insurance?

T : Full insurance, please. Can I have a road map?

R : Sure. Fill out this form, please. How do you want to pay?

T : Master Card. please.

R : Go easy with your driving and be aware of our traffic that keeps to the left. Here is your key and receipt. Have a nice trip.

T : Thank you.

2) 렌터카 직원과의 대화(B)

T : Traveler	**R :** Rent-a-Car Office's Staff

T : I'd like to rent-a-car today.

R : Yes, sir. Do you have an international driver's license?

T : Yes, but I usually use my Seoul license.

R : That's good. What kind of car would you like, a four-door sedan or a hardtop?

T: I think a hardtop. What are you rates?

R: Here's a list of the charges.

T: Are insurance and tankful of gas included?

R: Of course.

T: OK. The hardtop will be good.

R: Will this be charged to your credit card or cash?

T: I'll pay cash.

R: What time would you like your car?

T: I'll want to use the car from nine in the morning to six in the evening.

4 버스에서의 안내

(1) 호텔로 향하는 도중 현지 여행사 직원의 안내

T: Tour Conductor **L**: Local Agent

L: Good morning, everyone. Welcome to New York. I'm very glad to meet you. I'm Young Soo Kim from Global Travel. I really hope you have a wonderful time here in New York. I shall be happy to be of any service to all of you. Thank you very much.

T: Thank you, Mr. Kim. How long does it take from the airport to the Hilton Hotel?

L: It takes about 50 minutes.

T: It's away from here a bit, isn't it?

L: Yes. This is the new itinerary for you. Please review it. If you have something to change, let me know.

T: Thanks for your kindness. I will.

버스 안에서의 안내사항에 관한 회화

1. I'll have all the baggage put in the trunk compartment of the bus.
2. (To the tour conductor) Pleases it in the back. I'll sit up front to direct the driver.
3. This bus is driven by a very experienced driver. The traffic is a bit heavy, but the knows best route to the hotel.
4. Your hotel is very near. It can be reached in 30 minutes, depending on traffic
5. Is this your first visit to this place?
6. We are going to Hilton Hotel over the expressway No.7.
7. Soon we'll pass by a newly reclaimed land. From this land fill our skyline looks very good.
8. This is the Time Square, one of the busiest areas of this city
9. Now, we'll soon be able to see Twin Building, one of the famous landmark of this town. Behind the building is a train marshalling yard.
10. In a few minutes, we are arriving at Hilton Hotel, we'll park in front of the main entrance of the hotel.
11. I'll have the driver place the baggage at the door of the hotel.
12. Also, I'll arrange for the bell captain to take care of your bags.
13. As for your money change, the hotel cashier will always be at your service.
14. The hotel has a main dining room on the 2nd floor. Grillroom for a la carte menu is located on the 1st floor. Coffee shop will be found in the 1st floor. Bar is next door to the coffee shop.
15. You need to wear a coat and tie in the dining and grill room, but at the

coffee shop you can dress any way you like.

16. Postage stamps are obtainable at the vending machines installed in the arcade in the lower level.
17. Travel information including rent-a-car service is a vailable on the street.
18. Efficient laundry service is available from 9 a.m. through 4 p.m. except Saturdays and Sundays.
19. The hotel has 8 elevators, 6 for express and 2 for local services.
20. Check-out time of the hotel is 12 o'clock in the morning.

1. 수화물 전부를 버스 트렁크에 실어두겠습니다.
2. (TC를 향해서) 뒷좌석에 앉으세요. 저는 앞에 앉아서 운전사를 유도하겠습니다.
3. 이 버스는 숙련된 기사가 운전하고 있습니다. 교통은 좀 지체되고 있지만 운전사가 호텔까지 가는 가장 효율적인 길을 알고 있습니다.
4. 호텔은 가깝습니다. 교통사정에 따라 다르지만 30분 정도면 도착하겠습니다.
5. 이 지역은 처음입니까?
6. 고속 7호선을 따라 힐튼 호텔로 향하고 있습니다.
7. 잠시 후 새로 만든 매립지를 통과하겠습니다. 이 매립지에서 보이는 스카이라인은 아름답습니다.
8. 이곳은 타임 광장으로 이 거리의 가장 번화한 지역의 하나입니다.
9. 자, 쌍둥이 빌딩이 보이기 시작했습니다. 이 시의 유명한 건물입니다. 이 빌딩 뒤쪽에 열차주차장이 있습니다.
10. 곧 힐튼 호텔에 도착하겠습니다. 호텔 정면 입구 쪽으로 주차하겠습니다.
11. 운전사에게 짐을 호텔 입구 쪽으로 옮기도록 하겠습니다.
12. 벨 캡틴에게 여러분들의 수화물을 옮기는 것을 돕도록 하겠습니다.
13. 여러분의 환전에 대해서는 호텔 캐셔가 항상 서비스할 것입니다.

14. 호텔에는 2층에 대식당이 있고, 일품요리의 그릴룸은 1층에 있습니다. 커피숍은 1층에 있습니다. 바는 커피숍 옆에 있습니다.
15. 대식당과 그릴룸에서는 코트와 넥타이를 착용해야 하지만 커피숍에서는 자유복장입니다.
16. 우편은 지하 아케이드에 있는 자판기에서 구입할 수 있습니다.
17. 렌터카를 포함한 여행정보는 1층에서 이용할 수 있습니다.
18. 세탁 서비스는 토 · 일요일을 제외한 9시에서 4시까지 이용할 수 있습니다.
19. 호텔에는 8개의 엘리베이터가 있는데 6개는 급행이고, 2개는 로컬 서비스입니다.
20. 호텔 체크아웃 시간은 오전 12시입니다.

American Customs

Throwing Rice at Newlyweds

The custom of throwing rice at newlyweds derives from a Pagan rite of showering the happy couple with grain. A Roman wife was married with wheat sheaves and, with her husband, ate a post-ceremonial cake made of wheat. The wheat sheaf and cake were meant to impel bliss and to ensure fertility, since it was believed that the fertility of the seeds would be transferred to the pair on whom they fell.

A: I must say that I admire Sarah's fortitude. What four kids and another on the way, I don't know how she does it.

B: I know what you mean. Do you suppose that shower of rice at the wedding might have helped things along?

A: Who knows? There might be something to that old belief that the fertility of the rice is transferred to the wedded couple.

B: It appears that Sarah is living proof that it's true.

American Superstitions

Protectors of the wedding couple

The bridesmaids and ushers once dressed like the bride and groom to trick evil spirits so that they would not know who was getting married. Later, the job of the ushers was to stand watch during the honeymoon. Nowadays, bridesmaids and ushers are simply friends who help the bride and groom during the wedding celebration.

A: Virginia, have you picked out your bridesmaids yet?

B: Yes, I have. I've asked five of my best friends, and Bill is asking five cousins to be ushers.

A: Wow! That's a large wedding party.

B: Maybe, but for such a special day we want all the help we can get.

* 자료 : 《101 American Customs》 《101 American Superstitions》에서 발췌

Chapter 3

호텔에서의 영어

체크인

호텔에 도착하면 먼저 프런트 데스크로 가야 한다. 체크인하는 동안 여행객을 현관에서 기다리도록 안내한다. 프런트 데스크 직원들이 룸의 종류 및 체크아웃 시간 등을 안내하므로 이를 확인하고, 이때 귀중품이나 고액현금 등은 금고에 맡겨 보관하는 것이 좋다. 이곳에서 호텔 예약확인서나 호텔 예약확인 등이 필요하므로 체크인 수속을 밟아야 한다. 이때 예약확인서와 여권을 제시하여 호텔 투숙자 등록카드를 작성하면 된다. 체크인 때는 방이 없는 경우와 예약한 방과 틀릴 경우에 문제가 발생하기 쉽기 때문에 주의한다.

체크인을 끝마치면 벨맨들이 여행용 가방 등을 가지고 손님을 룸으로 안내한다. 대개 일류호텔들은 도어맨이나 벨맨들이 손님을 친절히 맞으며, 룸서비스맨들이 객실 내의 불편한 사항이나 요구사항 등을 친절히 서비스해준다.

식사 서비스

아침 이른 시간에는 외부 식당은 영업을 하지 않으므로 아침식사는 대개 호텔 식당을 이용한다. 메뉴를 보면서 주문할 수도 있겠으나 주로 뷔페로 되어 있는 아침식사를 든다.

룸서비스

호텔에 있으면 여러 가지 룸서비스를 부탁할 때가 있다.

분실물

기본적으로 체크인할 때 수하물의 개수를 확인해두면 물건이 분실되는 경우는 없다. 각 단원의 방에 운반되어 있는 짐은 본인이 책임져야 하기 때문에 우선 단원의 방부터 조사할 필요가 있다.

체크아웃

벨 캡틴과 프런트의 사전연락이 가장 중요하며, 체크아웃 때에는 영수증의 금액을 잘 확인하고, 메시지의 유무를 확인하고, 방의 열쇠를 반납한다.

1 예 약

(1) 호텔 객실 예약

1) 호텔 직원과의 대화(A)

T: Tour Conductor   O: Operator   R: Reservation Clerk

O: Hilton Hotel. May I help you?

T: Good morning. Give me the reservation desk, please.

O: Just a moment, please. I'll put you through to Advance Reservations.

R: Good morning. Hilton Hotel Advance Reservations. Can I help you?

T: Yes. I'm a tour conductor. I'd like to make a reservation for my members.

R: All right, sir. What day will you arrive on?

T: We'll arrive next Monday, the 29th of September.

R : Monday, the 29th. And for how many nights do you want the room?

T : We'll be there for five nights.

R : What kind of room would you like?

T : I want to have twelve double rooms and six single rooms, please.

R : Yes. It's available.

T : Is it with a bath?

R : Double room has a bath, but single room has a shower.

T : That's OK. And can we get a room with a view of the sea?

R : Oh, I'm sorry, but there is no view of the sea. Instead we have quiet rooms, sir.

T : OK, I'll. Could you tell me what the rate is?

R : The double room charge will be $85 per night and the single room charge will be $75 per night. Would that be fine?

T: Are service charges and tax included?

R: Yes, sir.

T: Good. That would be fine.

R: OK, May I have your name and phone number?

T: Kim. And my phone number is 02-555-6482.

R: OK, Mr. Kim. Thanks for your booking. Please let me know if there are any changes. We look forward to seeing you soon.

2) 호텔 직원과의 대화(B)

T: Tour Conductor **O:** Operator **R:** Reservation Clerk

O: Walker Hill. How can I help you?

T: Hello, reservation office, please.

O: Thank you. I'll connect you with the reservation desk.

R: Reservation desk July speaking. Can I help you?

T: Yes, I'd like to reserve a single room for three nights from January 21st to 24th.

R: Wait a minute, please. Yes, that's fine. May I ask your name and phone number, please?

T: Yes, My name is Kim. Phone number is 497-6829.

R: Thank you for calling.

3) 호텔 직원과의 대화(C)

T: Tour Conductor	R: Reservation Clerk

R: How can I help you?

T: Yes, I'd like to reserve a single room.

R: Yes, sir. When would you like to reserve it?

T: For tonight. Do you have rooms available?

R: Yes, we have some.

T: I'd like an inexpensive room.

R: We have one on the fourth floor that's near the stairs.

T: Isn't that noisy?

R: A little. But it is fine that soundproofing has gone well.

T : OK. I'm so tired I think I could sleep in the street. I'll take it.

R : All right. How many nights will you be here?

T : Two nights. But can I just take that room for tonight and change tomorrow if it really is too noisy?

R : Of course. And you can check-out 12p.m.

4) 호텔 직원과의 대화(D)

T : Tour Conductor	**R :** Reservation Clerk

R : Reservation desk, Woma speaking. Can I help you?

T : Yes, I'm phoning from the airport here in Boston. I'd like to reserve a twin room, for about 80 dollars a night. Monday to Thursday night. Do you have accommodations available at that price?

R : Yes, we have one.

T : Oh, good.

R : May I ask your name?

T : My name is Jun-ho Kim.

R : Would you spell that, please?

T : My last name is spelled K-I-M. My first name is spelled J-U-N-H-O.

R : Thank you, sir. What time will you be arriving?

T : Soon. I'm taking the airport limousine into the city. By the way, could you tell me the best place to get off to reach the hotel?

R : Sure. Go right to the bus terminal and take a taxi from there. That's the best way.

5) 호텔 직원과의 대화(E)

T : Tour Conductor	**R :** Reservation Clerk

R : Reservations, July speaking. How can I help you?

T : Yes, I'd like to reserve a room for 8 adults and 9 children for the 29th of January.

R : How long do you plan to stay?

T: For 4 nights.

R: OK. We could give you a twin room and put an extra bed in it. Would that be suitable, sir?

T: That would be fine. By the way, what would the charge be?

R: How old is the child?

T: Two are elementary school students the others are under 7.

R: Well, there would be 10 dollars extra charge per night under 7, and elementary school student charges half of adult fare. So, including breakfast the charge would be 150 dollars per night.

T: Good.

(2) 호텔 객실의 예약이 안 되었을 경우

T: Tour Conductor	**F:** Front Desk Clerk

F: Good morning. May I help you?

T: Yes. I want to check in.

F: OK. May I ask your name?

T: My name is Kim from Happy Tour.

F: Just a moment, sir. Oh, I'm sorry, but I can't find your reservation on our computer. When did you make a reservation, sir?

T: Oh, no. My travel agency must have made a reservation a week ago. It was the Happy Tour of Seoul. Are you sure it's not there?

F: I'll check again, sir. I'm sorry but we don't have your reservation.

T: Our members came to visit New York. Do you have any rooms available?

F: No, sir. I'm afraid we're booked up today.

T: Oh, no. It's terrible! I was sure they'd done it for me. Well, What can I do?

F: Wait a moment, sir. I'll call the manager. I'm sure he'll be able to suggest something for you and your members. Perhaps there'll be a cancellation today.

T: I hope so.

F: Have a seat over there, please. When he can't find a vacant room, he is willing to recommend another hotel for you.

2 체크인

(1) 호텔 체크인 중 객실 수가 잘못 예약되었을 때

T: Tour Conductor	**F:** Front Desk Clerk

F: May I help you, sir?

T: Yes I'm the tour conductor of the Happy Tour, and we've just arrived. We're supposed to have reservations.

F: We've been expecting you, sir. You are the Happy Tour party, right?

T: Yes. We are.

F: Are you Mr. Lee?

T: No, I'm Kim. He is the boss in my travel agency.

F: Oh, excuse me, Mr. Kim. Welcome to Hilton Hotel.

T: Thank you.

F: A party of thirty-two?

T: Oh, no. It's thirty.

F: We are holding eleven double rooms and ten single rooms for thirty-two people.

T: Something is wrong. We had requested twelve doubles and six singles through Happy Tour, and It's been booked. The voucher also say twelve doubles and six singles. Total is thirty people.

F: All right, sir. I'll give you room twelve doubles and six singles for thirty, and rooming list.

T: Thank you.

F: We're very sorry, sir, but two of the doubles I just gave you has no bath.

T: Oh, It's terrible! Don't you have any other rooms with bath?

F: We're are very sorry, but all other available rooms are with shower only.

T: Is that room with shower?

F: Yes. It's with shower, but no bath. Would you please take this room just for today? We certainly will change the room for you tomorrow, sir.

T: Please be sure to change this for a room with bath tomorrow.

F: Of course, sir. We're sorry to inconvenience you, sir.

T: That's okay.

F: Are you going to stay with us for five nights?

T: That's right. We'll check out on Friday.

F: Very well. Shall I put your room on the master account?

T: Sure. Now it's all set, right?

F: Thank you a lot, sir. Here are your keys.

T: One key to a room?

F : No. One key to each guest.

T : Thank you.

(2) 호텔 체크인(A)

T : Tour Conductor	**F :** Front Desk Clerk

F : Good afternoon. May I help you, sir?

T : Yes. I'm the tour conductor of the Happy Tour.

F : Nice to meet you, sir. May I have your name?

T : Kim. Kim is my last name.

F : All right, Mr. Kim. Do you have reservation letter?

T : Here it is.

F : You have made the reservations from the Global Travel in here. And also you reserved twelve double rooms, six single rooms for you from Sep. 29th to Oct. 3rd. Is it correct, Mr. Kim?

T : All right.

F : Would you fill in this registration form, please?

T : Sure. Here it is. When shall I pay for it, now or at check out time?

F : You shall pay for it at check out time. How are you paying?

T : By Traveler's checks. And could I get a wake-up call for tomorrow at 7:00?

F : OK, sir.

T : Thank you a lot.

F : Late checkout time is 3:00, with a charge of $25. Here's your room key, sir, and the bellman will carry your baggage. Have a good day!

(3) 호텔 체크인(B)

T : Tour Conductor	D : Doorman
F : Front Desk Clerk	B : Bell Captain

T : Please call porters. We have thirty baggage to be taken into the hotel.

D : Certainly, sir. Porters are here now. I'll ask them to bring in all of your bags.

T : Thank you. Could you tell me where the front desk is?

D : Go straight ahead and step down. The front desk is right in front of you.

T : (To a front clerk) Who is in charge of group checking in?

F : Just a moment, sir. I'll see if he's in. There he is. Peter! your client is waiting for you at the desk.

F : Good morning, sir. I'm Peter Pan handling group checking in. May I help you?

T : Good morning Mr. Pan. I'm the tour conductor of Happy Tour from Korea. My name is Kim. We have room reservations here by Global Travel Service's Chicago office.

F : One moment, please, sir. Let me check our records. Here it is. It says you are a party of thirty with thirteen twins and four single rooms each with bath?

T : Yes. That's our party. Here is the rooming list.

F : Are there any changes in the room list?

T : No, no changes so far. Are all rooms the same size? I'd like to make sure of that before I pass out room keys to our members.

F : Yes, sir. They are all same in size.

T : Great, now give me the room keys. please

F : Here they are, four keys for singles and twenty-six keys for thirteen twin rooms. I'll have the bell captain bring your bags to the rooms.

B : I see all of your bags have blue tags. I'll take care of them.

T : Very good. We have two Kim's on the rooming list.

Don't mix them up.

B: No, sir. We won't.

(4) 예약 변경을 하지 않았을 때의 체크인

T: Tour Conductor **F:** Front Desk Clerk

T: We lost three members. We have now twenty-seven people altogether. We should have informed you of this in advance, but we didn't have any time to contact you on the way.

F: I see. How many rooms do you need now?

T: We need twelve twins and three single to make a total of fifteen rooms.

F: Can you tell me the final shape of the rooming list?

T: Yes, please cross out the name on the second line from the top, also the name on the second and third lines from the bottom should be omitted from the roster.

F: What about the room assignment?

T : Mr. Park originally registered to use a single room, now wants to double up with Mr. Yoon. In other words, Mr. Lee who cancelled to join the tour was now replaced by Mr. Park who shares the twin room with Mr. Yoon. We give up one twin and one single.

T : (Some time later) One of my group members, Mr. Choi, is complaining that his room is too noisy. His room is 1462. facing the main road. There's too much noise from the traffic. Can you change his room?

F : We're filled up on the fourth floor. What about a room on the fifteenth? It's a larger quieter room, overlooking the residential area, but it's a little bit more expensive.

T : How much will it be the extra?

F : Five dollars per day more.

T : We shall be here for three days and paying you eight hundred dollars for our accommodations. Do you think this five dollars should be your expense, not ours?

F : I'll let you know as soon as I talk to our manager.

T : In the meantime, when he can change the room?

F : Could you wait for about ten minutes? I'll fix it up.

T : Please call me in ten minutes,

F : Now Mr. Choi may move to Room 1516 on the fifteenth floor and there will be no additional charge.

3 객실 배정

(1) 벨 캡틴과 변경된 방에 대해 이야기할 때 사용하는 회화

T : Tour Conductor　　　**B** : Bellman Captain

T : Hello, Captain. I'm the tour conductor.

B : Yes, sir.

T : This is our baggage. How many pieces did you receive?

B : I thought it was thirty.

T : Good. Do you have your list there?

B : Yes, I got it here.

T : I want you to make a little change.

B : How do you want to change it?

T : Room fourteen seventeen has been added. Will you put Mr. Choi couple of fifteen twenty-four.

B : OK. Anything else?

T : That's all. Do you want me to help you put the room numbers on the baggage?

B : Thank you, but I've almost finished now.

T : How long will it take to bring up all the bags to each room?

B : It won't take more than half an hour because all the rooms except fourteen seventeen are on the same floor.

T : Will you please send them up at fast as you can?

B : Sure. We'll do our best.

T : Thank you.

4 벨맨 서비스

(1) 짐의 배달

T : Tour Conductor F : Front Desk Clerk B : Bellman Captain

F : I'll get a bellman to help you with your bags? Show Mr. Kim and his members to rooms.

B : Yes. Are these your bags, sir?

T : Yes. We are.

B : And other baggage coming, sir?

T : Yes. I've got six more pieces coming.

B : How many bags do you have?

T : Well. We have thirty bags.

B : Oh, I see. May I have your room keys, please?

T : Here you are.

B : Your rooms is on the 15th floor. Now, I'll show you to your room. This way, please. Watch your steps. Please take the elevator on your left, sir.

T : Thanks a lot. This is a nice hotel and this room looks nice.

B : Thank you, sir. Here we are, after you. Where shall I put your baggage, sir?

T : Over there by the window.

B : Yes. It commands a fine view of the lake. Let me show you this room, sir. Here is the light switch for the bathroom and the night table over there has all the switches for the room lights, radio, and air-conditioner.

T : OK. Very good.

B : The closet is here and the bathroom is in there. Right here is a refrigerator and mini bar fully stocked with liquor, beer and soft drinks. All stationery is in this desk drawer.

T : Are they complimentary?

B : No, sir. You'll be charged for what you drink when you check out.

T : OK. And how do I call the room service?

B : As for the telephone, please dial 9 for the front desk, 2 for the room service, and 3 for the bell captain. Room service menu and a brochure listening all the services of the hotel are on the desk. Our room service operates 24 hours, so please make use of it anytime.

T : Oh, I see. Is the bar still open?

B : Yes. The bar Terrace on the 1st floor serves until 11:40 p.m. Would you like me to reserve a table for you?

T : Oh, Yes, please. We want to have our break time in there at 8:00 p.m.

B : OK, sir.

T : Thank you. (offer money) Here you are.

B : I'm sorry, but we have a no tipping policy. There will be a service charge added onto your final bill.

T : OK. Thanks anyway.

B : It's my pleasure, sir. Just call if you need anything.

(2) 잘못된 짐의 배달

T: Tour Conductor	B: Bellman

B: (Knocking at the door) Good afternoon. Your members' baggage is here, sir.

T: Yes. Please come in.

B: I have thirty pieces. Please check it that is all, sir.

T: Yes. That's all we have. Let me check. Oh! two of them isn't ours.

B: Are you sure, sir? It come with the other two pieces.

T: No. I'm sure it's not ours. They are all with yellow tags, but it has a different tags. Perhaps you've made some mistake, I guess.

B: I'm sorry, sir. It's probably our mistake. I'll go down and check with the bell captain. And I'll be back with the correct ones right away.

T: OK. Please hurry up. By the way, does the room door lock itself?

B : Yes. It does. So don't forget to take your key when you leave the room.

5 체크아웃할 때의 짐 서비스

T : Tour Conductor	**B :** Bellman

B : Good morning, bell captain. May I help you?

T : Yes. I'm tour conductor. We're getting ready to leave. Will you send someone up to my room 1512 for our baggage? All baggage is in my room.

B : Sure. Right away, sir.

(A bellman immediately goes up to room 1512 and takes all of the guest's baggage down to the lobby)

B : Is this all your baggage, sir?

T : Yes. Thirty baggage is all. Check it again, please.

B : It's correct. Shall I call a taxi for you?

T : No, thank you. We'll take our bus and please take all of the baggage to the bus?

B : OK. Have a nice trip and please come back again.

T : Thank you.

6 객실 내에서의 여러 서비스

(1) 장거리 전화 서비스

T : Tour Conductor **O :** Operator **L :** Long Distance Operator

O : Operator. May I help you?

T : This is Mr. Kim, in room 1512. I want to place a long distance call to Chicago, please. Are there special night rates from here?

O : Yes. The night rates are from eight in the evening until six in the morning.

T : What time is it in Chicago now?

O : There is a time difference of one hour. It's eight twenty there now.

T : Good. I'd like to make a call in now.

O : OK. Wait for one moment. I'll connect you with the long distance.

T : I don't want the call to put on my bill. I want to charge it on my credit card.

O : OK. What is the number of your card?

T : It's 27138298, Master Card.

O : Thank you, sir. I'll get the long distance and report the charges to you later.

T : Can I get the call through right now?

O : I think so. But if the lines are busy, you may have to wait a little.

T : I can't wait long. I'm in a hurry. We have to go out.

O: OK. Just a minute. I have a long distance call now. Hold the line, please. Long distance. Mr. Kim, room 1512 of the Hilton Hotel, wants to place a long distance call. He wants to charge it to his credit card.

L: Who do you want to call, Mr. Kim?

T: I'd like to call Mr. Choi in Chicago, area code 773, number 619-6489. Charge it to my credit card.

L: Hang up, please. I'll call you back in a few minutes. (A few minutes later) Here is your party in Chicago, Mr. Kim. Go ahead, please.

(2) 모닝콜을 부탁할 때

T: Tour Conduct	O: Operator

O: Operator. May I assist you?

T: This is Mr. Kim of Happy Tour. Can you give our members a morning call at 6:30 a.m.?

O: Yes. Mr. Kim. Morning call at 6:30 a.m. Have a nice sleep.

T: Thank you.

(3) 하우스키핑

1) 객실을 청소하기 위하여 하우스키퍼가 방문할 때

T: Tour Conductor	**M:** Maid

M: (Knocking on the door) Hello? Is anyone in here?

T: Hah? Yes? What's the matter?

M: May I come in to make up the room?

T: Oh, no. Not now. Please come back in another hour. I'll go out at 11 o'clock.

M: Yes, sir. Sorry to disturb you.

T: That's OK. I should put out the "Do not disturb" sign.

M: Yes, sir. Then you won't be disturbed. If you want to make up your room, put out the "Make up the room" sign, please.

T: OK. I'll. Anyway thank you.

2) 메이드 서비스를 부탁할 때

T: Tour Conductor	H: Housekeeping Clerk

H: Housekeeping. Can I help you?

T: Yes. Please send someone to my room.

H: Yes. What's your room number, sir?

T: Fifteen-twelve. I'd like the bathroom cleaned up.

H: Yes, sir. A maid will be there right away. Anything else?

T: I want two bath towels. And please send someone fix the desk lamp in Mr. Lee's room fourteen-seventeen. It seems to be a little dim.

H: I'll have them sent up to your room and Mr. Lee's right away, sir.

T: Thank you. And Could you get Mr. Lee's child an extra bed cover and blanket, too?

H: Of course, sir.

T: Very good. Thanks a lot.

(4) 세탁 서비스

1) 세탁물을 서비스받을 때(A)

T : Tour Conductor	L : Launderer

L : Good morning. This is housekeeping. May I help you?

T : This is Mr. Kim, tour conductor in room 1514. Some of my members want laundry service. There are all laundry in my room. Would you please send someone to pick up their laundry?

L : Yes, sir. I'll send someone right now.

T : What shall I do?

L : Please put your laundry in the laundry bags and write your laundry item in laundry and dry cleaning slip.

T : Where are the laundry bags?

L : You will find them with the slips in the closet.

T : Oh, I see. If we send out laundry today, when can we get it back?

L : Are you in a hurry?

T : No. But we must leave here the day after tomorrow morning.

L : Usually you can get it back the next day. But if rushed, you can get it in the evening. There in an extra charge, though.

T : There is no rush.

L : OK. I'll send someone to your room right away. (After a while) Laundry service! Good morning, sir.

T : Come in. You wait here as it won't take me long to fill this out.

L : Sure, sir.

T : Here they are. Two jacket, three blouses and five pants. You'd better check it to see if it is correct.

L : (After recounting) You have three blouses written, but I only have two.

T : Really? Let me check them again. Oh, the other blouse has dropped on carpet. Now, here it is. Is it right?

L: Yes, it is correct, sir. You say you are not in a hurry?

T: No. It'll be done tomorrow afternoon, won't it?

L: Yes, about five p.m.

T: OK. Please don't fail to remove this stain on this blouse.

L: What stain is this?

T: It may be chili sauce stain.

L: Um, I'll see what I can do, sir.

T: I hope you will do a good job.

2) 세탁물을 서비스받을 때(B)

T: Tour Conductor	**L:** Launderer

T: Good morning. I'm in room 1872. I'd like to have two shirts and some underwear laundered and a suit cleaned and pressed. Can you send someone up soon?

L: Yes, sir. Right away.

T: And when can I have those things back?

L: We can get the suit back to you by tomorrow morning,

using regular service, the laundry will be ready by 5 tomorrow evening. Will that be all right?

T: That's fine.

L: Well be right up.

3) 세탁한 세탁물을 받을 때(C)

T: Tour Conductor	**L:** Launderer

L: Good afternoon. Laundry service, sir.

T: Come in.

L: I have brought your laundry.

T: Have they done a good job? Did chili sauce stain remove?

L: Yes. I believe you will be satisfied. Would you check the laundry please? Here is the laundry, slip you signed yesterday. Please have a close look at it.

T: I believe it's correct. (After checking his laundry) Yes, it's correct. Thank you.

L: It's my pleasure. Here's your laundry bill. How will you be paying?

T : By hotel voucher. Where can I sign it?

L : Here you go. Sign here pleasure. Thank you.

7 안내 데스크에서 안내를 받을 때

T : Tour Conductor **I :** Information Clerk

I : Good morning, sir. Can I help you?

T : Yes. I want to get my digital camera repaired. Is there a repair shop near here?

I : Camera repairs are done by the hotel's gift shop. Go just along the corridor to the flower shop and you can see it by the Grand bar.

T : Really? That's very convenient. By the way, our members want city tour. Do you want to make arrangements for a city tour bus?

I : Of course, sir. I can take care of that for you. How many people are there in your party?

T : There are thirty people.

I : Here is a brochure of sightseeing bus tour.

T : Thank you. How much is it?

I : That depends on what kind you wish to take. The morning tours from nine to noon are priced at 30 dollars. The afternoon tours from one to four cover a few more places. The charge for those is 35 dollars. And the night tours from seven to eleven are priced at 50 dollars.

T : What is difference of afternoon tours and night tours?

I : Night tours are the most popular. They include theaters, bar, and other such places at cut-rate prices.

T : Well, thanks for all the information. I'll study this brochure carefully and decide which tour to sign up for.

8 호텔 내에서의 식사

(1) 아침식사

T : Tour Conductor	W : Waiter

W : Good morning. May I take your order, sir?

T : Yes. I'll have this American breakfast combination.

W : OK, sir. What kind of juice would you like? We have orange, tomato, mango juice.

T : I'll have mango juice.

W : OK. Next, you get two eggs cooked as you wish. Boiled or fried?

T : Fried, please.

W : Sunny-side up, or over-easy?

T : I'd like my eggs sunny-side up.

W : OK. And you have a choice of sausage or bacon.

T: I'll take bacon. Make sure it's good and crisp.

W: Yes, sir. And which would you like better, mashed potato or cereals?

T: What kinds of cereals do you have?

W: We have corn flakes, shredded wheat, puffed rice, and oatmeal.

T: I'll have oatmeal. And would you make my toast light.

W: Yes, sir. Coffee or tea?

T: Tea with milk, please. And please rush my order. I have to be at the airport by nine a.m.

W: All right, sir. I'll bring your order right away.

(2) 룸서비스로 주문시

1) 룸서비스로 아침식사 주문시(A)

T: Tour Conductor	**R**: Room Service Clerk

R: Room Service. May I help you?

T: Hello, am I too late to order from the breakfast menu?

R: No, sir. The room service menu is available twenty-four hours a day.

T: Good. Then can I have one English breakfast?

R: Sure, sir. Cereal or fruit juice?

T: Orange juice, please.

R: There's coffee and tea. Which would you prefer?

T: White coffee, please. And two cheese burger with onions, no French fries, three BLT(bacon, lettuce, tomato) sandwiches, and a ham and egg sandwich.

R: Two burger and onions, three BLT and one ham and egg sandwiches. Anything else, sir.?

T: Some drinks please. Five Ice tea and three bottles of plain soda.

R: All right. What is you room number, please?

T: Room 1415.

R: 1415. It'll be about fifteen minutes, sir.

T: That's great. Thank you.

2) 룸서비스로 아침식사 주문시(B)

T: Tour Conductor	**R:** Room Service Clerk

R: This is Room Service. May I help you?

T: I'd like to order a ham sandwich and a cup of coffee. This is Mr. Kim in room 1209.

R: Thank you very much. It will take about 15 minutes. (knocking on the door) Is this Mr. Kim's room? This is Room Service.

T: Yes. Please come in. The door isn't locked.

R: Good morning, sir. Your breakfast is ready. Where would you like to eat?

T : Please put everything on this table.

R : All right, sir. Here you are.

T : And I also want to keep the tea hot.

R : The tea is in this electric percolator. If you plug this cord into the wall socket, it will stay hot.

T : That's fine.

R : Would you please sign this slips, sir?

T : Sure. Here it is. What should I do with the dishes when I finish eating?

R : Please leave them outside.

T : Thank you. This is for you.

9 호텔 안에서 물건을 분실했을 때

T: Tour Conductor **C**: Lost and Found Section Clerk

C: Good afternoon, sir. May I help you?

T: Yes. Mrs. Shin, one of my members, has lost her wedding ring. Might it be in your lost and found section?

C: Well, I can check, sir. What kind of ring and what does it look like?

T: She said, it made of white gold and blue sapphire. Also, it is heart shape. Her name and her husband's are printed in it, and the ring is the one what she received from her husband. So her really want to get it back.

C: Oh, It's very important ring. Just a minute, sir. I'm sorry, but I'm afraid we don't have any ring at all. Is she sure she didn't leave it in her room?

T: Yes. She looked all over for it in her room, and it's not there. And when she went out her room to go shopping, she was wearing the ring in her finger.

C : Where did she go shopping?

T : At the hotel shopping arcade. And after shopping, she went to the hotel fitness center.

C : Don't worry. Please fill out this lost article report and I'll make sure a contact you if it's found.

T : Please help her find it.

C : Yes. We'll do our best. (one hour later) Hello, Mr. Kim. this is the lost and found section clerk. Good news. Mrs. Shin dropped the ring in dressing room of fitness center, and they are keeping it in the safe.

T : Oh, Thank you very much for your help. I'll go down and pick it up right away, and She wants to stop by at your desk to thank you personally.

C : Oh, not at all. But I'll be most happy to meet her at my desk.

T : Thank you again. See you soon.

10 체크아웃

(1) 체크아웃(A)

T : Tour Conductor	**F :** Front Desk Clerk

F : Good morning, what can I do for you?

T : Yes. When is my check out time?

F : Twelve o'clock p.m., sir. Are you checking out today?

T : Yes. I am the tour conductor of Happy Tour. But our flight isn't until this evening. Could we use the two rooms until 5 o'clock?

F : I'm sorry, sir. But if you don't check out by twelve p.m., then you'll have to pay a one-day extra charge.

T : Oh, no. I can't afford that. We need the rooms only 5 hours. Can't you make a special arrangement only for us?

F : Sorry, sir. But it's our hotel's policy. I'm afraid I can't break it. You'd better speak to the manager about it if you wish.

T : Um. If we check out as soon as possible, can you watch our baggage for us until this afternoon?

F : Of course, sir. Just give your baggage to the bell caption over there. He'll take care of it for you.

T : All right. I'll do that.

F : I am sorry not to give you big help.

T : That's OK. Anyway, thank you a lot.

(2) 체크아웃(B)

T : Tour Conductor　　**F :** Front Desk Clerk

F : Good morning, sir. Can I help you?

T : Yes, I'm ready to check out now, room 872.

F : Fine sir. I'll print out your bill now. Did you enjoy your stay here?

T : Yes, I did very much. I'll come back again.

F: Thank you, sir. Here's your bill.

T: Good. Do you take credit cards?

F: Sure, sir.

T: What kind of credit cards do you take?

F: We take all kinds of credit cards.

T: Here's Master Card.

F: Please sign here. Would you like a call taxi to the airport?

T: No, thank you. I'll take the airport bus.

F: OK, Thank you very much for staying at our hotel.

(3) 체크아웃시 정산

T: Tour Conductor **F:** Front Desk Clerk

T: I'm the tour conductor of Happy Tour. I'd like to check out now, please.

F: Very good, sir. I'll get you your bill. Here it is.

T: Oh, thank you. Let's have a look at it now. Oh, no. It's a lot more than I expected.

F: Would you like me to explain any items, sir?

T: Yes. What's this charge for eight dollars marked 'L'?

F: 'L' is a charge for a long distance telephone call, sir. Did you make a telephone call that night?

T: Yes. I don't forget now. Oops, we must have talked for a long time. And these ones, 'R' and here's another, 'B', what are they for?

F: 'R' is for room service. Perhaps you used the laundry service or got something from the room service.

T: Yes, right. I did get some laundry service, and I got some juice and burger from the room service.

F: 'B' stands for breakfast.

T: Ah yes. As I know, breakfast is included in the price of the room.

F: Yes, you're right, but you did get special meal.

T: Oh, I see. I forgot.

F : And you may find some other meals marked also, here you have an 'L' for lunch and a 'D' for dinner.

T : Oh. I think the bill must be right. Thanks for explaining everything.

F : It's my pleasure, sir. How would you like to pay, sir? Credit card?

T : Yes, credit card.

(4) 체크아웃시 짐의 운반사항 문의

T : Tour Conductor **F :** Front Desk Clerk **B :** Bell Captain

T : Can you take care of our baggage that goes out tomorrow noon at check out time?

B : Yes, we can, but I'll be off tomorrow noon, and Simon, one of our porters, will handle your baggage.

T : Then, will you tell Mr. Simon that we have thirty bags to be picked up at 9:00 tomorrow morning?

B: Certainly, I will. I'll make a note of the items to take care of.

T: Please start collecting our baggage at 9:00 a.m. The baggage will be placed at our room doors. All of our seventeen rooms are on the 15th floor. Our rooms are, as you see in the rooming list, from 1549 through 1567, 1583 and 1586.

B: Very good, sir. Anything else?

T: Our hand-carry bags will be on the beds. Don't take anything off the beds. Our members will carry their own hand baggage themselves.

B: (To front desk clerk) We are going to check out tomorrow noon. Please have all bills, including incidentals and others, ready by 9:00 a.m. tomorrow morning.

F: Will you have lunch here tomorrow, sir?

T: Yes, the account for the lunch will be settled with the coffee shop direct, so no check for the lunch will be included in the master bill.

F: Yes. I understand, sir. Your account will be ready at 9:00 a.m. in the mourning at the latest.

T: We'll clear all our account at 9:00. By the way, is it possible for you to offer us a spare room for two hours after the checkout time? Our bus will leave here for airport at twelve o'clock tomorrow afternoon. We don't like to wait in the lobby for two hours.

F: I think that can be arranged. Let me see how many hospitality rooms will be available tomorrow at noon.

T: I certainly appreciate your help.

F: (At the cashier just before the check-out time) We have your account here ready now, sir. Will you please check all the bills.

T: Very will, wait a minute, here's an item I don't agree with you. It's five dinners on the evening we arrived here. We checked in here very late in the evening. How could we eat these three dinners? The check has a Korean signature and his room number which are unknown to us. This is not our party.

F: Let me go over it. Oh, yes, we inadvertently put this into your bill. I'm sorry. I'll take this amount out of your bill right away. Here's a fresh bill for you.

T: Now I see the bill all right. Now, I'm turning in the rooms keys. Thirty of them in all.

호텔에서 사용하는 회화

1. I made a reservation in airport information center.
2. I'll stay here five days and four nights.
3. Is there a room available tonight?
4. You reserved four double rooms, two twin rooms, and one single room for you from May. 25th to 29th.
5. Wake up call, please. Morning call at 6 o'clock, please.
6. I'd like to make an international call to Paris, please.
7. Please take this brochure. It'll give you all the information the facilities of our hotel.
8. Room service menu a brochure of the hotel are on the desk.
9. I'll send someone up there with them.
10. I want to have english breakfast tomorrow morning around eight o'clock.

1. 공항 안내센터에서 예약을 했습니다.
2. 여기에 4박 5일 동안 머물 예정입니다.

3. 오늘밤 사용할 수 있는 객실이 있습니까?

4. 5월 25일부터 29일까지 더블룸 4개, 트윈룸 2개, 싱글룸 1개를 예약하셨습니다.

5. 모닝콜 부탁합니다. 6시에 모닝콜 부탁합니다.

6. 파리로 국제전화 부탁합니다.

7. 이 브로슈어를 보시면 호텔 시설에 관한 모든 안내사항이 있을 것입니다.

8. 호텔의 룸서비스 메뉴는 책상 위에 있습니다.

9. 직원을 그곳으로 보내겠습니다.

10. 내일 아침 8시에 영국식 아침식사를 준비해주십시오.

American Customs

The Man Walks on the Outside

When a man and a woman walk together, convention dictates that the man walk on the curb side of the street. The practice probably originated because the man needed to protect his female companion from runaway horses and street brawlers, and from other hazards of the street, such as the garbage being hurled onto the street from upper-story windows.

A: Careful, Kathy. Keep away from the curb or you'll get splashed.

B: I'm sure I'll be well protected from all the elements with you walking next to me. After all, you have always been the perfect gentleman.

A: Thanks for the compliment. I'm glad to see that you appreciate a good man when you see one.

B: Okay, Boris. Don't get carried away.

American Superstitions

Throwing salt over the left shoulder

Because humans and animals need salt for life, spilling salt was considered a serious misfortune and a sign that evil spirits were trying to take away the household's salt. To avoid them, you should throw a pinch of salt over your left shoulder because that is the side where the spirits live.

A: Mario, you've spilled salt all over the table. Now you're throwing it over your shoulder and onto the floor. Why are you making such a mess?

B: Spilling the salt on the table was an accident. Grandma says if I throw some over my shoulder I won't have any more accidents, and I'll always have salt for my food.

* 자료 : 《101 American Customs》 《101 American Superstitions》에서 발췌

Chapter 4

관광과 쇼핑

관 광

인솔자는 시내관광 출발 전날 방문하는 장소와 목적에 따라 필요한 소지품과 적절한 복장 등에 관해서 정보를 제공해야 한다. 시내관광 전에 현지 여행사에 대하여 미리 연락방법, 관광버스 배차시간 등을 미리 알아두어야 하며, 가이드나 운전기사와 협의하여 최종적인 여행 코스(관광지, 소요시간, 식사, 휴식)와 하차 장소, 인환증의 기재사항과 관광지의 내용 체크 등을 결정한다.

통상적으로 시내관광은 이미 합의되어 있는 일정에 따라 행하는 것이 상례이다. 그러나 현지 가이드에게 일임해버리면 단체의 성격이나 희망사항 등을 고려한 충실한 관광이 안 될 수도 있으므로 최종적인 결정을 인솔자가 내리는 것이 중요하다.

배차시각은 출발예정 시간보다 10~15분 정도 전으로 정해둔다. 단원의 수에 의해 차량 대수와 차종을 확인한다. 관광 코스에 대해서는 전체적으로 코스에 무리가 없는지 식사예약의 확인, 후식장소의 시간, 특히 화장실에 대해서는 단원의 인원 수, 인원구성에 대해서 충분한 배려가 필요하다. 인환증과 관광지에 써 있는 것은 하나하나 확인한다. 다음으로 입장료, 식사요금 등이 포함된 경우를 체크한다.

관광당일에 확인할 사항은 관광버스 배차위치의 재확인, 가이드는 운전사 겸 가이드인지 본인에게 확인한다. 그리고 코스를 재확인하고, 출발해서는 예정대로 여행이 진행되는지 체크한다. 또한 관광지에서는 관광 종료 후 집합시간과 장소, 경우에 따라서는 식사, 화장실 등의 장소를 확인한다.

쇼 핑

쇼핑은 해외여행에 있어서 커다란 즐거움 중의 하나이다. 인솔자는 여행객들이 조금이라도 기분이 좋고, 보다 좋은 물건을 구입할 수 있도록 배려해야 하며, 너무 지나치게 고가의 물건을 산다든지 많은 물건을 사서 외화를 낭비하지 않도록 적절한 조언도 잊지 말아야 한다.

쇼핑시에는 다음과 같은 점을 염두에 두고 업무에 임하도록 한다. 특산품, 상품의 품질, 특색, 판매가격(한국과의 비교), 상점의 규모, 평판, 상점의 영업일과 시간, 이에 대해서는 토요일, 일요일, 국경일, 개점과 폐점시간, 휴식시간의 유무를 확인한다.

또한 통용되는 언어의 확인, 사용화폐, 수표, 신용카드를 확인한다. 또 상점과 백화점에 따라서는 물품을 고르는 곳과 대금 지불하는 곳이 있다. 이러한 사항들을 인솔자는 사전에 잘 정리하여 투어의 전반적인 흐름 속에서 적절한 기회를 잡아 안내한다.

1 관광 전의 여러 의논사항

(1) 에이전트 사원과 의논

1) 당일 여행을 갈 경우 현지 에이전트 사원과의 미팅

T: Tour Conductor **R**: Representative of Local Agent

T: Good morning. I'm Kim, tour conductor of Happy Tour from Korea.

R: Nice to meet you, Mr. Kim. I'm Lee of Global Travel in New York.

T: Nice to meet you, too. Shall we seat over there and check the tour program?

R: Yes. (Showing a copy of tour itinerary to Mr. Kim) This is a full-day excursion to Washington.

T: When and where does it start?

R: We'll pick you up at the hotel at 8:00 a.m.

T: When do we come back to the hotel?

R: You will come back about 6 p.m.

T: Good. Is it far from here?

R: No. It isn't. It takes about 40 minutes by bus.

T: OK. Good.

2) 엑스카션의 구체적인 미팅 바우처 내용을 체크하면서 이야기를 진행한다

T: Tour Conductor **R:** Representative of Local Agent

T: How long does it take from here?

R: It's a long drive. Maybe it'll takes about 4 hours.

T: Do we stop over somewhere on the way to Washington?

R: Yes. You'll take a rest at Philadelphia some 40 miles from here. then continue for another 40 miles to Washington. At Washington you'll visit the Luray Caverns. I'm sure it will be an interesting experience for your group, even for a person who dislike cave.

T: How long we stay in the Cavern?

R: About an hour.

T: Sounds interesting. What about lunch? Do we eat lunch around Luray Caverns?

R: Yes. Just after the Caverns tour. We reserved the Market Inn. It's a clean and inexpensive sea food specialty store. It'll takes about 20 minute by bus from the Caverns.

T: Your voucher says, no lunch is included in your arrangements. In other words, we'll have to pay the Market Inn direct, won't we?

R: Yes. That's right.

T: Do we have to book tables at the Market Inn?

R: I made a reservation at 1:00 p.m. for your group. The restaurant service will not be rushed it's off the peak lunch hour.

T: Fine. What can we see in Washington?

R: Well, as shown in the itinerary you'll see the White House, Smithsonian Museum, Washington Monument and

Jefferson Memorial.

T: What does the city tour fee include? Are the admission fees for those places included in our tour fare?

R: No. They're not. You pay your account at these establishments yourself.

T: How much is the admission fee for the museum?

R: It's one fifty for an adult.

T: OK. Can you have our bus parked at the hotel 7:30 a.m. tomorrow morning.

R: Sure. I'll see you tomorrow morning.

(2) 가이드, 운전사와의 의논

1) 가이드 서비스 내용 확인

T: Tour Conductor　　**G:** Guide

G: Good morning. Welcome to New York. I'm Lee from Global Travel. I'm the driver and guide. I'm very glad to meet you.

T : Glad to meet you, Mr. Lee. My name is Kim tour conductor of Happy Tour.

G : I really hope you have a wonderful time in Washington today. I shall be happy to be of any service to all of you.

T : Thanks a lot. Where can I see our bus?

G : It's in the garage of this hotel.

T : Good. Mr, Lee. Shall we leave here at 7:30?

G : Right. Do your members speak English?

T : No. Not all of them. They may understand what you say when you speak slowly. I'll tell them in Korean what you have said.

G : Good. We'll have tour in Washington after lunch. In the morning I'll tell you all about the Civil War in this country on the way to Washington. It takes about 4 hours ride from here.

T : That'll be an interesting lecture tour for us. When you are talking about historical items, try not to speak too much. Please pause for a few minutes in between, so I can easily translate into Korean. Can you do that?

G : Yes. I can.

T : Everyone's here now. We can start now.

2 관 광

(1) 사전 관광예약

T : Tour Conductor	E : Travel Agency Employee

T : Tour reservation here?

E : Of course. How many people can go?

T : 25 people, we'd like city sightseeing information.

E : OK.

T : How can I go?

E : By tour bus.

T : Do you have some guidebooks in Korean?

E : Sure. Do you want guidebooks?

T : Yes, and recommend some places to see around here.

(2) 목적지에 도착해서 관광을 어떻게 진행시킬 것인가를 가이드와 미팅

T : Tour Conductor	**G :** Guide

G : We are now at the Washington. First of all, we shall visit the information center to see an outline map of Washington.

T : What else we can see at the information center?

G : You can buy an official guide book and also see a free orientation film in Korean.

T : In Korean?

G : Yes. The orientation is taped in 6 languages including

Korean.

T: Can we get a brochure for Washington?

G: Yes. You can now, we'll get off the bus. Bus will be locked, but please don't leave any of your belongings in the bus.

T: No, We won't.

3 쇼 핑

(1) 쇼핑의 기본적인 회화

S: Store Clerk	**K:** Korean Traveler

S: May I help you?

K: Excuse me, where can I buy a camera?

S: The electronics department is on the seventh floor. As you get off the escalator you will see it on your left.

K: Where is the escalator?

S: Go straight down the hall. You will find it on your right.

K: Thank you so much.

(In the electronics department)

S: What are you looking for?

K: Can I see that camera for a minute?

S: Sure, you mean this one?

K: Yes, and show me another one, please.

S: Here you are.

K: Thank you. What's the difference between these two?

S: This one is automatic and that one is hand-operated.

K: What are the prices of these two?

S: This on is $300 and that one is $200.

K: I'll take this one.

S: Good. Cash or charge?

K: Charge, please.

S: OK. Do you have an ID card?

K: Yes. Here is my passport.

S: Please sign your name here.

K: OK. Could you wrap it?

S: Take it to that counter, please.

K: Thank you.

(2) 조금 복잡한 쇼핑의 경우

S: Store Clerk	**T:** Traveler

S: May I help you?

T: Yes. I'm looking for a shirt.

S: What's your size?

T: A medium size, please.

S: How about this one?

T: Sorry, that's not what I want. Do you have the same one in different colors?

S: OK. How about this color?

T: Let me try it on.

S: There is a fitting room over there.

(After a while)

S: How does it fit?

T: It's too tight around the waist. Show me some more.

S: OK. Could you wait for a moment? I think this one becomes you.

T: This fits me well.

S: Good. Anything else, sir?

T: That's all today. How much is it?

S: That'll be 75 dollars.

T: Oh, it's too expensive. Can you come down on the price?

S: Sir. This is twenty percent off the price.

T: I can't afford it. The limit of my budget is seventy.

S: OK. We'll give you another five percent off the price. This is really our rock bottom price.

T: OK. I'll take it.

S: Please pay the cashier over there, thank you.

T: Thank you so much.

(3) 쇼핑 후 물건의 문제 발생

S: May I help you?

T: Yes. I bought this camera yesterday. But it doesn't work. Can I have a refund on this? Here is the receipt.

S: I'm sorry, sir. We don't refund the money. But you can exchange it for another one with the same price.

T: All right. I will exchange it for another.

(4) 편의점에서의 쇼핑

T: Tour Conductor **C:** Convenience Store Employee **P:** Passer

T: Excuse me, where can I buy a tooth brush?

P: You can buy it at the convenience store.

T: Is it the nearest a convenience store from here?

P: Yes, it is Seven-Eleven around the corner.

T: Thank you very much.

(In the convenience store)

T: Excuse me, where can I find a tooth brush?

C: It is in the aisle 5 on your left. It is next to the school supplies.

(5) 쇼핑 후 선물 포장과 배달

T: Traveler	**E:** Store Employee	**C:** Cashier

E: Anything else?

T: That's all. I'd like to have this gift-wrapped.

E: Please take it to that counter.

C: What kind of paper do you want?

T: It's for my son's birthday. What paper do you recommend?

C: How about this color?

T: That's good. And I'd like to have this delivered to the Hilton Hotel.

C: OK.

관광과 쇼핑에서 사용하는 회화

1. Is there something particular you're looking for?
2. I'm just looking for a jacket for me.
3. What size do you wear?
4. May I try it on?
5. Can you give any discounts, if I buy two?
6. Would you mind taking a picture for me?
7. Excuse me, how do I get to the Metropolitan Museum?
8. Where is the nearest subway station?
9. Let me off here, please.
10. I think this is my seat.

1. 특별히 찾으시는 것이라도 있으십니까?
2. 자켓을 찾고 있습니다.
3. 사이즈가 어떻게 됩니까?
4. 한번 입어봐도 됩니까?
5. 만약 두 개를 사면 할인해줄 수 있습니까?
6. 사진 좀 찍어 주시겠습니까?

7. 실례하지만 메트로폴리탄 박물관으로 가려면 어떻게 갑니까?

8. 가장 가까운 지하철역이 어디에 있습니까?

9. 여기서 내립시다.

10. 이 자리는 제 자리인 것 같습니다.

American Customs

Bacon and Eggs

Bacon and eggs(or sometimes sausage of ham) is the traditional American breakfast. It is a throwback to the colonial days when pigs were easy to keep because they could forage for themselves. Eggs for breakfast were ideal because they were at their freshest when gathered from the previous night's roosting. In colonial times pigs and chickens were the easiest animals to transport. Although the opening of the west made beef king, the colonial mania for bacon and eggs persists even after the setting of the west and the end of the frontier.

For years Chris had always eaten a hearty breakfast of bacon and eggs; however, when the doctor told him that the would have to change his diet for health reasons, he didn't take too kindly to having oatmeal instead. After all, he felt that a grown man needed "fitting nourishment" to keep up his strength.

American Superstitions

A two-dollar bill

In the United States the two-dollar bill is considered unlucky since it is a reminder of the two or deuce in a deck of playing cards; "deuce"is an old name for the devil. To change the bed luck, the corner of the bill should be torn off.

A : Paul, can you lend me some money?

B: All I have is this two-dollar bill. Do you want it?

A: Sure. I'll tear the corner to be safe. Then maybe I'll get lucky and my paycheck will come early.

* 자료 : 《101 American Customs》 《101 American Superstitions》에서 발췌

Chapter 5

방문과 연극 · 영화 등의 관람

회사와 지인 등의 방문

어느 경우에도 문서 등에 의한 사전준비와 재확인이 필요하다. 회사(공장) 방문에 필요한 체크포인트는 견학할 때 그곳의 책임자와 담당자의 확인, 처음 방문하는 사무소와 접수처의 장소의 확인, 복장 · 휴대물 등의 체크, 최종 인원 수의 보고, 인사와 이야기 등의 연락 등이 있다.

① 견학하는 곳의 책임자에 대해서는 왕복문서의 서명자가 책임자로 되어 있을 경우에는 틀림이 없지만 실제로는 담당자가 지명되어 있는 경우가 많다. 담당자는 대체로 광고(PR) 인사관계에 있다.

② 사무소의 장소는 왕복문서 받는 곳의 관청과 회사의 주소에 도착하는 것이 필요하다.

③ 장소에 따라 캐주얼 복장이 좋을지 체크한다.

④ 최종 인원 수는 인솔자도 포함한 인원 수를 보고한다. 회사방문 등의 경우에는 전원에 대한 점심을 제공하는 것이 많기 때문에 최종 인원 수의 연락은 견학처와 협력한다.

⑤ 견학하는 곳에서 강연 등이 예정되어 있는 경우에는 이름, 직급, 주제, 소요시간 등을 연락해둔다. 지인을 방문할 때에는 시간을 우선하고 방문일시를 사전에 미리 정한다.

관 람

대개의 도시호텔의 안내계와 벨 캡틴이 있는 곳에서는《금주의 뉴욕》과 같은 가이드북이 놓여 있기 때문에 이것을 이용하면 좋다.

1 공장 견학

(1) 견학시 주의사항

Now for some information regarding the plant tour. As it is now scheduled you should reach the plant a little before 9:00 a.m. and the tour will be completed by 12:00 noon.

Ours is a large plant and the team members should wear their comfortable walking shoes. You probably are aware that our plan is a defense plant and hence we have important security regulations to which we must conform. Will you please inform team members and everyone talking the tour that.

① They will not be permitted to take photographs or even carry a camera into a plant.

② Tape recorders or other means of recording are also forbidden.

③ In order to tour the plant each person must wear an identification badge. These will be prepared before you arrive.

④ When touring the plant the party will be divided into two groups and a guide will be provided for each group.

These groups must stay with their guide at all times. My office is in the plant and if you need to call me on Monday my office telephone number is 543-2943 or 543-2543 and can be dialed directly from chicago telephones. My home telephone number is 743-1832.

Don't hesitate to call If I can be of assistance. We are looking forward to meeting with the team and to their visit to our plant

(2) 공장 방문의 의논에서 견학 순서, 시간, 통지서의 내용을 전화로 재확인

T : Tour Conductor　**O :** Officer　**M :** Mr. Young

T : Hello, is Mr. Young in? I mean, David Young, the plant manager.

O: Yes, he is. May I ask your name, Please?

T: I am Mr, Kim, and I'd like to talk to him about the pre-arranged plant visit.

O: Hold on, Mr. Kim.

M: Mr, Young speaking.

T: Mr. Young? I am Mr. Kim. I'd like to double-check with you some items about the plant visit for tomorrow.

M: Yes, I have a letter from 'Kyungmin Culture Tourism Industry Research Center' that you are coming here tomorrow morning.

T: Could you tell me how to reach your plant I'm now in the Hilton Hotel.

M: Oh, are you? Then, drive along the Nelson Highway until you come to Evandale Point. The landmark will be an old brick building with a Chevy Ad on the roof located at the junction of Nelson Highway and Evandale point.

T: Yes.

M: There turn to the left and continue driving for about 10 minutes and our plant is on the right side. You can enter our plant through Gate 2. When you come to our plant, first see Mr. Garnon, Personnel Manager at the reception office. He will tell you what they can do for you.

T: Very well. Nows peaking of the arrival time, I have your notice which says that we have to be there before 8:30 a.m. right?

M: Yes, exactly.

T: Then, we'll manage to arrive at your plant around 8:00 a.m.

M: That'll be fine, Mr. Kim. Anything else?

T: I have some problems.

M: You do? What are they?

T: All of our members are taking cameras with them because in the afternoon we'll go on a sightseeing tour in the town. Your notice says no camera are allowed.

M: No problem. Just bring your cameras along. Mr. Garnon will take care of those cameras when you check in at the reception office and he'll keep them while you are on a on a plant visit with us.

T: That's very kind of you, Mr. Young.

M: You're welcome

T: Other items in your notice have already been told to our team members. They are no tape recording, putting on walking shoes, and our group will be split into two smaller groups and will follow your assigned guides.

M: Exactly, Mr. Kim.

T: Very well, then, I'll be seeing you tomorrow morning Mr. Young.

M: Fine, thank you for calling, Mr. Kim.

(3) 지인 방문의 확인과 미팅

1) 면회의 약속과 시간 약속

T: Tour Conductor **S:** Mr. Smith(travel agent in the USA)

T: Hello, Mr. Clint, this is Mr. Kim, tour conductor of

group traveling in the USA.

S: Well, Mr. Kim, what's on your mind?

T: I hope you remember me? I was at the PATA Conference in Seoul last winter. At that time, I promised you I'd provide you with some information about the destinations frequently visited by Korean travelers.

S: Mr. Kim, I remember now. We met at the Insadong Restaurant in Seoul on a very cold winter day. 1 enjoyed the Bulgogi dinner there very much.

T: Yes. I've brought a report with me. In it, there are more than a dozen destinations in the USA with total numbers of Korean who visited these sites.

S: Really. It's very kind of you, Mr Kim.

T: I am planning to give the report to you tomorrow. We are staying here for a couple of days and I will find time tomorrow at lunch.

S: Sorry, but I have a previous appointment for tomorrow's lunch. What about after 6 tomorrow evening?

T : I can find time after 7:00. Dinner would be excellent. Is it too late for you?

S : No, 7:30 is quite all right. Shall we meet at 7:30 at the Hamilton? Their beef steak is excellent.

T : Very well, Mr. Clint. Then, I'll be at the Hamilton at 7:30 tomorrow evening. I'll tell you all about the movement of Korean travelers tomorrow.

S : I hope so, see you tomorrow evening. Thank you for calling me, Mr. Kim.

2 영화 · 연극 신청시의 회화

(1) 호텔종업원에게 상영영화 및 영화관의 일반적인 사항 문의

T: Tour Conductor　　**H**: Hotel Clerk

H: Good afternoon. May I help you?

T: Yes. I'd like to attend the theater this evening with all the people of my group. What play is putting on the stage? Will you do one recommendation?

H: Yes. As this Theater Guide shows, the Broadway theater is running a film, "Cats". There's another film, "Phantom of Opera".

T: What's popular now?

H: It's "Cats".

T: Sounds interesting. Where can I buy tickets?

H: You can buy the tickets at the theater box office as soon as you get there.

T : When do they start showing those plays in the evening?

H : At 4 and 7 o'clock. The first show has already started. I suggest you take in the second performance which begins at 7:00 in the evening.

T : Thank you. We'll be there around that time.

(2) 호텔종업원에게 콘서트 좌석 예약 부탁

T : Tour Conductor   H : Hotel Clerk

H : Good afternoon, sir. May I help you?

T : Yes. We'd like to go to a concert this evening. Can you reserve a seat for us?

H : Yes, sir. We can reserve a seat for you at the Broadway theater in the 5th avenue.

T : What's on the program at the theater?

H : The program includes Beethoven Leonore Overture No. 3,

Mozart Piano Concerto No. 20 in D minor, K.466, Beethoven Symphony No. 7 in A major, Op. 92.

T : I see. Please reserve ten seats for our members.

H : Very well, sir. The concert start at 6 p.m.

T : OK. By the way, can you tell me the way to the theater?

H : Shuttle bus of the theater may come to pick up you and your members at 5:30 p.m.

T : Very good.

(3) 인기를 끌고 있는 공연 티켓은 구하기 어렵다. 사전에 수배가 필요하다.

T : Tour Conductor	**TE :** Theater's Employee

TE : Good afternoon? Which tickets would you like?

T : Good afternoon. Thirty tickets for "Cats" for seven o'clock.

TE : For today?

T : Yes.

TE: Which seats do you want?

T: I want thirty seats in the first row near the stage, please.

TE: I'm sorry but the first row is full., end row only.

T: Oh, no. We can't see in the end row for it isn't seen well.

TE: This play is performing continuously during 2 months. On this week Thursday, the first row remains.

T: OK. Please book us 30 tickets at 7 p.m.· on this Thursday.

TE: That'll be three hundred dollars.

T: Here it is.

TE: Check your tickets, please.

T: Yes. Everything is exactly.

(4) 인기 있는 경기 표는 당일에는 판매하지 않기 때문에 예매를 해야 한다. 한국과 같이 암표상이 나타나기도 한다.

T: Tour Conductor **TE**: Theater's Employee **TB**: Illegal Ticket-Broker

T: Can I buy game tickets now?

TE: No. They are sold out.

T: Isn't even standing room only?

TE: No.

TB: Sir, I've got some tickets for today. You need some, don't you?

T: Yes. I need the tickets. How much do I owe you for the tickets?

TB: It's 50 dollars per ticket.

T: That's too expensive. Why is it too expensive?

TB: It is trade. Why don't you take the chances?

T: I don't buy the tickets.

TB : The ticket box office opens at 11:00 in the morning. You'll have to line up at that time for the next day's tickets.

T : Do we? I'll come here tomorrow morning to get the advance tickets, anyway. Thank you for your advice.

TB : You're welcome.

American Customs

Garage Sales

Garage sales, or lawn or yard sales, are as big a part of American culture as apple pie and popcorn. Periodically, people clean out excess clothing, furniture, appliances, etc. from their homes and display the goods for sale to passersby, either on their front lawns or in their garages. The goods are always sold at greatly reduced prices, since getting rid of unwanted goods is more important than realizing even a modest profit from the sales.

A: Louise, what are you planning to do with that old lamp and coffee table?

B: I hope that I can get a little something for them at the garage sale I'm planning for this Saturday.

A: Hey, I've got some things I'd like to get rid of, too. How about we do it together at my place since my garage is bigger?

B: No problem. I'll have my husband clear out the rest of the stuff from the attic while we're at it.

American Superstitions

Hanging clothes from a doorknob

An old custom was to hang clothes from a doorknob of a house or room as a sight that someone inside had died. When there has been no death, hanging clothes from a doorknob would invite misfortune.

A: Please take your coat off the door and put it away.

B: But I always hang my coat on the doorknob.

A: Not today. I'm making dinner for my friends, and I want everything to go well.

* 자료 : 《101 American Customs》 《101 American Superstitions》에서 발췌

Chapter 6

레스토랑에서

레스토랑에서 식사를 할 경우에 단체예약이 필요한 것은 말할 나위가 없다. 예약은 전화로 하는 것이 가장 일반적이지만 장소가 가까우면 그곳까지 가서 예약을 하는 것이 가장 좋다. 예약을 할 때 필요한 것은 상식적이지만 인원 수, 식사시간, 좌석준비, 인솔자의 이름 등이다. 인원 수가 미확인일 경우에는 인원 수보다 많은 인원을 알려준다. 그리고 레스토랑으로 출발하는 직전에 최종 인원을 알려준다.

식사 시작시간은 종료시간과 관계 있지만 30분 정도 시간의 여유를 둔다. 식사 시작시간은 메뉴 종류의 선택에 따르기 때문에 메뉴는 인솔자에게 맡기는 것이 좋지만 사전에 단원의 의향을 들어두는 것도 필요하다.

또한 좌석준비는 단체의 경우는 테이블을 붙여두는 경우가 많다. 이름과 동시에 연락방법도 알려준다.

레스토랑에 도착하면 우선 휴대품 보관소에 코트 등을 맡기고, 웨이터의 지시에 따라 좌석에 앉는다. 좌석에 앉으면 웨이터가 음료수 주문을 받는다. 레스토랑에 따라서는 음료수 전문 웨이터를 와인 스튜어트라고 말하며, 일반 웨이터와 구별하는 경우가 있다. 식전의 술은 칵테일, 와인, 맥주 등이 있고 알코올 음료는 식후 술이다.

1 레스토랑의 예약과 주문

(1) 레스토랑의 좌석 예약

T : Tour Conductor	R : Restaurant's Employee

R : Good afternoon, American Renaissance. How may I help you?

T : Hello, American Renaissance? I'd like to make a reservation for table at 7:00 p.m.

R : How many are there in your party, sir?

T : We are a party of 30 people.

R : Smoking or nonsmoking section?

T : Smoking, please.

R : Oh, I'm sorry, but the seats are full at that time. We can give you a table after 8:00.

T : OK. We'll be there at 8:00. Can we have table by the window?

R : I'll try. And may I have your name?

T : I'm Mr. Kim, tour conductor of Happy Tour.

R : That's a table for thirty, smoking, by the window, at 8:00. Is that correct?

T : Yes, Thank you. And Do you require a coat and tie?

R : It should be appreciated.

T : OK. We'll.

R : Thank you for calling, Mr. Kim. We'll be waiting for you at 8:00.

2 레스토랑 입구에서

(1) 예약을 했을 때

T : Tour Conductor	R : Restaurant's Employee

R : Welcome, come in. Do you make a reservation?

T : Yes, I do. I'm Mr. Kim of Happy Tour, for thirty.

R : Yes, Mr. Kim. Come this way, please. Here's nice table by the window. How about this table?

T : That's fine.

R : Do you expect anyone else to join you?

T : No, just thirty.

R : I see. Please take a seat. The waiter will be here in a moment.

(2) 예약을 하지 않았을 때

T : Tour Conductor	R : Restaurant's Employee

R : May I help you, sir? Do you have a reservation?

T : No, we don't. But do you have a table for thirty available?

R : We have four now, but Group seat should be available soon.

T : How long will we have to wait?

R : About fifteen minutes. Please wait here for a minute. I'll call your name when a table is available.

T : All right.

R : May I have your name, please?

T : Kim.

3 바에서 음료 주문

(1) 음료 주문시(A)

T : Tour Conductor   B : Bartender

B : Good evening, sir. What would you like to drink?

T : Give us five Whiskey, three Scotch, two bottles of beer and four cocktail, please.

B : How about trying Scotch on the rocks, sir?

T : What does Scotch on the rocks mean?

B : Rocks means ice. So it means straight Scotch with only ice and no mixer, sir.

T : Oh, I see. If we don't want any alcohol, what kind of cocktail do you recommend us?

B : I recommend you snow white. Snow white is made of peach and non alcohol.

T : OK. And if you don't want anything in your liquor, what

should you ask for?

B : Please just say, "I'll have a straight Scotch," or "I'll have two straight whiskies".

T : Give me a Scotch on the rocks, two straight Scotch and two straight Whiskies. And five cheese and crackers, and three nacho. How much is all?

B : One hundred twenty dollars, sir.

T : Here it is.

B : Thank you, sir.

(2) 음료 주문시(B)

T : Tour Conductor　　　**B :** Bartender

B : Would you like something to drink?

T : Do you have some kind of fruit juice?

B : Yes, sir. We have orange, tomato, mango and "blue peach" our famous.

T : That "blue peach" sounds good for me.

B : Fine. Would you like anything else, sir?

T : Another people will have cold beers. What kind have you got?

B : We have Tsingtao, Guinness, and Sapporo in bottles, sir.

T : Any dark beer?

B : No, I'm afraid we only have those three light beers.

T : OK, We'll take 3 'blue peach' and 12 Tsingtao.

(3) 음료 주문시(C)

T : Tour Conductor **B :** Bartender

B : Good evening, sir. We have Scotch, Tequila, Irish, Cognac, Rum, Gin, Vodka, Canadian and Liqueur. What kind would you like?

T : Well, I'll have a shot of Liqueur.

B : And you, sir?

T : I'll have Tequila.

B : And what would you like for a side-dish?

T : Well, no side-dishes.

B : I'm sorry but you should order side-dish from 8 p.m.

T : OK, what is?

B : We have chip and salsa, cheese stick and sausage.

T : I'll have chip and salsa.

4 간단한 주문 방법

(1) 식사 주문

T : Tour Conductor	**R :** Restaurant's Employee

R : Good evening. Do you have a reservation?

T : Yes. I made a reservation for eight o'clock this evening.

R : Can I have your name, please?

T : I'm Kim.

R : (Looking for his name in the list) Yes, Mr. Kim. I've got your name. Are all of your people here?

T : Yes, we're all here.

R : All right. I'll show you your table. This way, please. Is this table all right, sir?

T : Yes. This seat is very nice. I want to see the menu. I'll call you when we are ready to order.

R : Here it is.

(after a while)

R : Would you like to order now?

T : Which dish does the chef recommend?

R : Our chef recommend this course. This is today's special.

T : OK. I'll try it.

R : Would you like some drinks before dinner?

T : Yes, ten red wines, thirteen cocktails, seven beer, please.

R : What kind of beer would you have?

T : Please show me the beer list.

R : Here you are.

T : Thank you, We'll have this Miller.

R : What would you like for appetizer?

T : We'll have some shrimp cocktail for starters.

R : Very well, and soup?

T : We'll try eighteen cream of mushroom and twelve crab gumbo.

R : What would you like for the main dish?

T : All of us try the T-born steak. Does salad come with the steak?

R : Yes, sir. How would you like it?

T : Medium, please.

R : What kind of dressing would you like to have?

T : Thousand Islands, please.

R : What would you like for your garnish?

T: I'd like mashed potato and fried prawn.

R: Beverages?

T: Ten coke, fifteen coffee with cream and sugar and water.

R: Would you like anything else?

T: We'd like fifteen custard pudding and fifteen vanilla ice cream for dessert.

R: Very well. I'll be right back.

(2) 식사 전후의 간단한 음료와 디저트 주문

T: Tour Conductor	**R:** Restaurant Employee

R: Are you ready to order, sir?

T: I need some more time.

R: Would you like to have a cocktail?

T: Yes, Black Russian, please.

R: Would you like anything else?

T: Coffee will be fine.

R: Do you take cream with your coffee?

T: No, I like it black.

(after lunch)

R: What would you like to have for dessert?

T: What do you have?

R: We have cherry ice cream and all kinds of cake.

T: I'll have cherry ice cream. And I'd like to have a cup of tea with a slice of lemon.

R: What kind of tea would you like?

T: Do you have regular tea?

R: Yes, we have lipton tea.

T: That'll be fine.

(3) 패스트푸드점에서의 주문

T: Tour Conductor	**R:** Fast-Food Employee

F: May I take your order?

T: Yes, Five cheeseburgers, three large fries, two hash-potato, four big cokes and two small cokes.

F: Here or to go?

T: For here.

F: Will there be anything else?

T: Nothing.

F: What would you like on the cheeseburgers?

T: Hold the mayo and extra mustard, please.

F: OK, That'll be 35 dollars.

T: Here you are.

F: Here's your change. I'll be right back with your order.

T: And where are the straw?

F: The straws are over there.

5 레스토랑의 계산

(1) 계산의 전형적인 예

T : Tour Conductor	R : Restaurant Employee

T : Excellent food, delicious.

R : Thank you, sir.

T : Could I have the check, please?

R : Which would you prefer, separate bills or all in one?

T : One check, please.

R : Yes, sir. (after while) Here's the total amount, sir.

T : Is the service charge and tax included in the check?

R : Yes, all included.

T : Do you accept American Express?

R : Sure, No problem.

T : Here you are.

R : Your signature here, please.

T : Certainly.

R : Thank you very much, sir. And we hope to serve you again. Bye-bye.

(2) 식사 후의 계산(A)

T : Tour Conductor	**R :** Restaurant's Employee

R : Was you dinner satisfactory?

T : Everything was super.

R : Here is your bill. Your bill amount to two hundred fifty two dollars. It includes both the ten percent service charge and ten percent tax.

T : Do you charge Korean money?

R : Sure, sir.

T : What's the exchange rate today?

R : It's one thousand two hundred won to the dollar. Your amount comes to three hundred twenty thousand won.

T : Here is three hundred fifty thousand won.

R : Do you mind if I give you Korean change?

T : Of course not, no problem.

R : Here is your change, and receipt here. Please count it.

T : Thank you.

(2) 식사 후의 계산(B)

T : Tour Conductor	R : Restaurant's Employee

R : How did you enjoy your meal, sir?

T : Very excellent, thanks. Can I pay by check?

R : I'm sorry but we don't accept personal checks.

T : OK. I'll pay in cash. How much is the total?

R : Your total amount comes to 270 dollars.

T : Here are 300 dollars.

R : Thank you, sir. We received 300 dollars. Here is your

change and receipt.

T: Oh, I forgot to leave a tip on the table for the waiter.

R: Thank you, but we have a no tipping policy. Every tip is included in a 10% service charge which added to your bill.

T: Oh, I see.

R: Thank you, please come back again soon, sir.

계산시 사용하는 회화

1. I'd like the tab, please.
2. You can pay at the counter.
3. Waiter, where do I pay the bill?
4. I can take care of it for you whenever you're ready.

1. 계산서를 가져다주세요.
2. 카운터에서 지불하세요.
3. 웨이터, 어디서 계산하지요?
4. 손님이 준비되셨다면 언제라도 제가 계산해 드릴게요.

American Customs

Baseball-America's Game

One of the most distinctly American institutions is the game of baseball. The game is avidly followed by a great number of fans, either attending in person or watching on TV. Most of the time, the spectator's attention is focused on the batter and the pitcher. The game is not only practiced on a professional level, but on a local, suburban level as well.

Mrs. Smith had never been much of a Sports fan—unlike her husband and two children.

On weekends others would take in either a baseball or a football game, while she stayed home alone.

After a while the situation became a source of great annoyance to her.

One weekend, to the utter amazement of her husband and children, she announced that she wanted to attend the football game with them.

She thought, If you can't beat them, join them.

Mrs. Smith realized that since she could not talk her family out of attending the games, she might as well join them in one of their favorite pastimes.

By joining her family on the weekends she would alleviate her loneliness, and in time she might even come to like sports as much as her husband and children did.

American Superstitions

Hanging a horseshoe over the door

A horseshoe has always been considered a good luck charm. Some say this is because the horseshoe is in the shape of a half moon, a symbol of good fortune. Horseshoes often are hung over the door of a house of barn for protection.

A: How do you like our new house? We'll be moving in next week.

B: It needs just one more thing for the finishing touch. I brought you this horseshoe to hang over the door.

* 자료 : 《101 American Customs》 《101 American Superstitions》에서 발췌

Chapter 7

각종 문제의 처리

해외여행의 문제는 여정 이외, 예상외의 사태가 여러 가지 일어난다. 그러므로 여행자라면 누구라도 스케줄은 통고 없이 변경되는 것이라고 잘 알고 있다. 항공기의 불시착, 호텔의 화재 등이라고 하는 비상사태는 보편적인 것은 아니지만 예상하지 못한 상태, 항공기의 지연, 취소, 수화물의 행방불명, 도난 등은 꽤 많고, 손님의 발병, 교통사고 등의 생각하지 못한 사태도 때로는 발생한다. 그렇지만 그렇기 때문에 여행에는 인솔자의 존재가치가 있는 것이라 생각되어진다. 연이어서 일어나는 문제를 미연에 방지하거나 요령 있게 적절한 처리를 할 수 있는 것이야말로 인솔자의 역할을 발휘하는 것이라 할 수 있다. 통상 손님에게 발생하기 쉬운 사고나 문제에는 인솔자가 미리 주의를 주어야 하며, 항공회사에 체크하는 여행용 가방에는 현금, 귀중품을 넣지 않을 것, 생수는 마시지 않을 것 등은 일반 주의사항과 함께 잘 설명해야만 한다.

1 항공기

(1) 항공기의 지연

T: Tour Conductor **A:** Airline's Agent

T: This plane will be delayed for two hours, won't it?

A: I'm Sorry. The fog is so heavy that can't take off now.

T: When can you start?

A: The departure announcement will be made shortly.

T: If this flight is more delayed, We will miss my connecting flight to Seoul.

A: Don't worry, please. Estimated time of departure will be at two twenty.

T: We hope.

(2) 항공기 결항

T: Tour Conductor	A: Airline's Agent

A: Can I help you?

T: Can I have information of the fight 210 to New York?

A: Because it rains too heavy, the flight 210 to New York has been cancelled.

T: I have to be in New York by 6 p.m. tomorrow. Are there any other flights which get there by that time?

A: How many people are there in your party?

T: We are a group of 30 people and holding economy class tickets to fly to New York.

A: Hold on, please. We have a flighting leaving Philadelphia International Airport at 9 p.m. and we can set a side 30 seats for your group.

T: The arrival time should be Shortly after 5 p.m. local time.

A: Right. The flight is non-stop to Philadelphia International Airport. And Estimated Time of Arrival(ETA) will be

5:15 p.m. local time. Would you like to have the seats confirmed?

T: Yes, please. My name is Kim. Group's name is Happy Tour.

A: OK. Your flight number is 212 and It'll start at 9 p.m. Please be at airport before 7 p.m. Thank you for your calling.

(3) 긴급 착륙에 대비

1) 긴급 착륙에 대비한 문장

① If required, oxygen masks will be automatically preseted from a compartment in the overhead rack. Pull until pin is released. Unfold hose and bag from mask.

② Remain seated, do not smoke cigarettes must be extinguished immediately. Grasp nearest mask and pull it to your face. A cord turns oxygen on as you pull mask to you.

③ Promptly place the mask over nose and mouth. The oxygen supply tube is long enough to permit you to relax comfortably in your seat. For children's use, a spare mask is available at each row.

④ Put it on with a double bow at the side, pull red knob sharply down to inflate, top up by mouth tube. Do not inflate in the cabin.

⑤ To open the emergency door, rotate the handle counter-clockwise and push the door outwards. The slide comes out automatically.

⑥ Rough air at high altitudes can be severe. When seat belt sign is lighted in-flight, please comply with the sign to prevent possible injury.

⑦ Experienced air travelers usually leave their seat belts fastened all the time and pull them up snug when the seat belt sign is lit.

⑧ Familialize yourself with the location of the exits. Note particularly the exist nearest you. Study how they are opened.

⑨ Emergency position-remove shoes, eyeglasses and sharp objects from pockets. Take protective position.

⑩ When leaving the plane, do not take coats, purses or bags with you. Move to the exits immediately.

⑪ Jump on escape slide. Do not hold slides. From window exit, step out one leg first, then head and shoulders.

2) 불시착할 때의 기장 아나운스와 주의사항

(기장의 아나운스는 승객에게 불안을 주지 않는 것이 중요하다)

This is your captain speaking. Please listen carefully. We have a little trouble with our engines and we have to make an emergency landing in a few minutes. Please be assured that there is nothing to worry about and I would like your all to remain seated with your seat belt fastened. As soon as the aircraft has come to a completely stop, please follow the instruction of our flight attentions.

2 귀중품의 분실

(1) 분실한 화물을 찾아달라는 의뢰

T: Tour Conductor　　P: Police officer

T: Excuse me, officer.

P: May I help you, sir?

T: One of our tour members had his bag stolen.

P: When and where did you lose it?

T: He lost it on the eighth avenue while he was waiting for the bus half an hour ago.

P: What's in it?

T: He had traveler's check, credit cards, passport, and five hundred dollars in it.

P: Please make out a theft report. We'll contact you as soon as we find it.

T: We'll be staying at Hilton Hotel until this weekend. Please deliver the bag as soon as you find it.

(2) 여권을 분실하였을 때

T: Tour Conductor **P:** Passerby **E:** Embassy Employee

T: Excuse me. Can you tell me the way to the Korean Embassy?

P: Yes. Go straight and turn left at the second corner. You can see the Korean flag.

T: Thank you.

E: May I help you?

T: I lost my passport. I'd like to get it reissued.

E: When and where did you lose it?

T: I think I lost it at the subway around 1 p.m.

E: Please fill out this form and wait a moment.

(3) 신용카드 분실시 신고할 때

T: Tour Conductor	**C**: Card Company Employee

C: Master Card Company. May I help you?

T: I lost my credit card.

C: Don't worry. Would you tell me your name and card number?

T: My name is Kim, but I can't remember the card number.

C: No problem. I'll stop all your transactions. We've confirmed it and we'll make them issued.

T: Thank you.

3 의사를 부를 때

(1) 환자가 생겼을 때 의사가 오기까지 해야 할 응급처치에 대한 회화

T : Tour Conductor　　O : Operator　　C : Chemist

O : Hello, Operator.

T : This is 1106. a person of the room must be under the weather. Do you have a hotel doctor?

O : Yes. What symptoms does one have?

T : He has a very heavy fever.

O : OK. I will send a physician soon. The doctor may be available at this time.

T : Whew, what a relief! And where can I get some aspirin and a thermometer?

O : They are supposed to be sold at the pharmacy downstairs.

(in the pharmacy)

C : May I help you?

T : Please give me some aspirin and a thermometer.

C : Yes, just a minute. Here you are.

T : How many of these should I take?

C : Please take this one.

T : How do I use this thermometer?

C : Our thermometers are fahrenheit and to convert degrees fahrenheit into degrees centigrade, deduct 32, multiply by 5, and divide by 9. And it is oral.

T : Korea use it under the arm. Customs is different in the country.

(2) 건강 관리실

T : Tour Conductor	**D :** Doctor

D : What's the matter with you?

T : He has a stomachache.

D : When did his pain start?

T : He said, after breakfast today.

D : What did he eat today?

T : Chicken, fruit, ham and milk.

D : Does he have a disrrhea?

T : Yes.

D: (after check up) Don't worry. He just has indigestion. Take this prescription to the pharmacy.

T: Thank you a lot.

4 교통사고를 신고할 때

T : Tour Conductor   E : Emergency Agent

T : Hello. Is this 911?

E : Yes. May I help you?

T: There's been a traffic accident. Send an ambulance, please.

E: Are you the driver?

T: No. I'm a tour conductor from Korea. We were taking a picture of the George Washington Bridge and a truck hit us from behind and ran away.

E: OK. We'll be there right away.

T: Could you hurry, please? It is urgent state.

E: I'll. Are you hurt?

T: Yes. I have a broken arm. One of my members is bleeding from the head and fell unconscious. Three people who is involved in the accident, are bleeding from their mouth.

E: Oh, It is serious state. Take it easy.

T: OK. How long must I wait?

E: We'll arrive 2 minutes later.

5 호텔 객실에서의 문제 해결

T : Tour Conductor	H : Housekeeping Agent

T : Housekeeping, please.

H : Housekeeping. May I help you?

T : Room 707. I asked for hotel accommodation.

H : Sir, what's the trouble?

T : The room you gave me. I've never seen such a disgusting mess. What's the meaning of this?

H : I'm sorry, sir. We'll send someone right away. Could you tell me about the problem exactly?

T : The bed isn't made and the bath is filthy.

H : I see.

T : The toilet is disgusting and won't flush. Besides, the drainage is clogged.

H : I see. So that's both the bathroom and bedroom that are unsuitable for guests' use.

T : Exactly.

H : I'm extremely sorry about this. There's been a misunderstanding between the front desk and the housekeeping department. We seem to have given you a room which should have been marked down for thorough cleaning. What I'll do now is contact the front desk and make sure that you have a room that is fully up to standard.

T : I hope.

American Customs

"Trick or Treat" on Halloween

Halloween, also referred to as All Hallow's Eve, falls on October 31. It is believed that on this day, ghosts, spirits, and witches come out to harm people. In order to scare the evil spirits away, people place scary decorations such as black cats, skeletons, and ghosts in front of their homes. Children dressed in masks and colorful costumes go from door to door saying "trick or treat," and people give them candy, cookies, fruit, or money.

A: Let's get going, Judy. It's already getting dark. Sue is expecting us for trick or treating tonight.

B: I'll be right there. By the way, are you still going dressed as a wicked witch?

A: Absolutely. And how about you?

B: Probably just as myself. I don't have a costume.

A: That should frighten a lot lf people and get you a lot a treats. Mind sharing them with me?

American Superstitions

Lucky at cards, unlucky at love

According to tradition, a person cannot be lucky at everything. If he is lucky at cards, he will be unlucky at love.

A: Beth and Mario are the worst card players I've ever seen.

B: Yes, but they've been married for fifteen years. They're certainly lucky in love.

* 자료 : 《101 American Customs》 《101 American Superstitions》에서 발췌

Chapter 8

통신과 환전

전 화

전화회화는 짧게 용건을 정확하게 전달해야 한다. 중요한 것은 무심코 대답하지 말아야 한다. 예의상으로 대답한 Yes가 OK의 의미로 받아들여질 수 있다. 이것을 피하기 위해서는 상대방이 말한 것을 자기의 언어로 되풀이해서 상대방의 대화내용을 확인하는 것이 좋다. 회화는 요령 있게 처리하는 것이다. 결론을 먼저 말하고, 그 이유를 나중에 설명하는 것이 좋다. 또 너무 대화가 간단해지면 요점을 전달할 수 없다. 이것을 보완하기 위해서 회화 중에는 가능한 한 감사의 표현을 넣는 것이 좋다. 호텔의 교환수가 "무엇을 도와드릴까요?"라고 하는 경우에도 "예"만이 아니라 "예 부탁합니다"라고 하는 것이 에티켓이다.

우 편

메일에 관한 영어회화는 반드시 우체국뿐만 아니라 호텔의 메일데스크와 유럽 호텔의 관리인(Concierge) 사이에도 우표구입과 이메일의 유무를 둘러싼 회화가 많다. 여행지에 따라서는 우편사정이 나쁘고, 항공편도 일본에 가는 데조차 한 달 이상 걸리거나 호텔 종업원 중에서는 우표값을 손님에게 받으면서 우표를 붙이지 않고 보내는 경우도 있다고 한다.

환 전

간단한 말은 "Exchange this, Please"의 영어만을 알아도 괜찮다. 환율, 수표시세의 동향의 지식이 필요하다. 나라에 따라서는 재교환이 되지 않는 경우도 있다.

1 전 화

(1) 교환에게서 콜렉트콜 전화를 받는다

T: Tour Conductor　　O: Operator

O: Operator. How can I help you?

T: I'd like to make an international call to Seoul, Korea. Make it collect, please.

O: What's the phone number?

T: It's 02-555-6481.

O: Who would you like to talk to?

T: To Mr. Choi, please.

O: What's your name and number?

T: My name is Kim. The number is 714-865-7528.

O: Just a moment. (Mr. Choi? you have a collect call from Mr. Kim. Will you accept the charge?) Mr. Kim, The line is connected. Go ahead.

T : Thank you.

전화의 사용법과 전언

1. First remove receiver ; then deposit a quarter.
2. Pull out for dialing instructions, dia1 0 for operator, dial 9 for local calls dials. Wait for the dial tone and dial your number.
3. Telephone Message - the following message was received while you were out. - You aren't in the room. I'll call you back.

1. 처음 수화기를 들고 25센트를 넣어주세요.
2. 다이얼 지시를 따르십시오. 교환은 0번, 시내통화는 9번, 통화신호를 기다리고 전화번호를 다이얼해 주십시오.
3. 전화 메시지: 부재중일 경우 다음과 같은 메시지가 나옵니다. - 방에 안 계시네요. 내일 다시 전화하겠습니다.

(2) 외부에서 호텔로 걸려온 전화

O : Operator	**C :** Mr. Choi

O : Good afternoon, Hilton Hotel. May I help you?

C : Yes, please. I'd like to speak to Mr. Song of room 1752.

O : Hold the line please. Oh, I'm sorry, but Mr. Song is not the room. Can I take a message?

C : Yes. Could you tell Mr. Song that Mr. Choi called?

O : Sure. Does he know your phone number?

C : He's got my number.

O : OK. I'll give him the message.

C : Thank a lot.

(3) 외부에서 호텔로 잘못 걸려온 전화

O : Operator	D : Mr. Daniel

O : Hyatt Hotel, can I help you?

D : Yes, can I speak to Mr. Kim in room 9257?

O : Just a second, sir... I'm sorry but Mr. Kim isn't a guest of this hotel.

D : Oh, no. He told me to call him here. Could you check again?

C : All right, sir. Sorry but there is no one here by that name in any of our rooms.

D : Isn't it 6235-7248?

C : I'm afraid you have the wrong number. This is 6235-7240.

D : Oh, I've made a mistake. I'm sorry to have bothered you.

C : That's all right.

2 우체국에서의 회화

(1) 소포를 부칠 때

T : Tour Conductor	P : Post Officer

P : Good morning. May I help you?

T : To which window should I go to send this parcel?

P : Treat here.

T : I'd like to send this parcel to Seoul.

P : How would you like it sent?

T : By airmail, please.

P : What's in it?

T : Albums and magazines.

P : Korean customs seems to be very strict in observing the law against pornography. I have heard that no nude picture is allowed.

T : No pornographic magazines are in the parcel.

P : These are declaration forms. A customs declaration is required. Please, fill out this form.

T : OK. How much is the charge for this parcel post to Korea?

P : The rate is seventy cents a pound. Let's check the weight. Please put it on the scale. Seven dollars and fifty cents.

T : There. And I need two aerograms and five postcard, please.

P : The total amount is ten dollars and forty cents.

T : How long will it take to reach Korea?

P: Approximately 5 days.

T: OK. Thank you. And I'd like to have this parcel insured.

(2) 편지를 부칠 때

T: Tour Conductor	**P:** Post Officer

T: I'd like to send this letter by registered mail.

P: Where to?

T: To Los Angeles. How much is the postage on this?

P: For a regular size letter?

T: Yes. It's very light.

P: That will be 3.75 dollars.

T: What if I send it by express mail?

P: Then it would cost you 6 dollars.

우송에 필요한 것 구입시

1. How much is it for a postcard to Korea?
2. How much will it be by parcel post?
3. May I have some commemorative stamps?
4. Can I get boxes to pack this parcel?

1. 한국까지 엽서요금이 얼마인가요?
2. 소포로 보내면 요금이 어떻게 되나요?
3. 기념우표를 주시겠어요?
4. 소포용 상자가 있습니까?

호텔 프런트에서 우편물에 대해서 묻는다

1. Is there any message or mail for me?
2. Please forward mail to this address.

1. 내게 온 메시지나 우편물이 있습니까?
2. 우편물을 이 주소로 보내주십시오.

3 은행에서 환전할 때

T : Tour Conductor **S :** Security **B :** Bank Teller

T : Where can I change money?

S : Please follow me, I'll show you.

T : Thank you.

B : May I help you?

T : I'd like to exchange some money, please.

B : OK. How would you like it?

T : What's the exchange rate?

B : It's 1200 won to a dollar.

T : Please change the one hundred dollars to three twenties, three tens, one five, and five ones.

B : All right. Your passport, please.

T : There you go.

B : Wait a minute. Could you fill out this form and sign your name here? Please check your currency before you leave the counter.

환전할 때 필요한 회화

1. Please, change this ten dollars to all one dollar.
2. I want six ones, twelve quarters, nine dimes and two nickels.
3. Please, cash my traveler's check.
4. Can I get a cash advance with this credit card?
5. Please, endorse it on the back.
6. Give it to me in large bills.

1. 이 10불짜리를 모두 1달러로 바꿔주세요.
2. 1불짜리 6매, 25센트짜리 12개, 10센트짜리 9개, 5센트짜리 2개가 필요합니다.
3. 여행자 수표를 현금으로 바꿔주세요.
4. 이 크레디트 카드로 현금을 지급받을 수 있을까요?
5. 뒷면에 이서를 해주십시오.
6. 고액권으로 주십시오.

American Customs

Gathering for Thanksgiving Dinner

Thanksgiving is celebrated throughout the United States on the fourth Thursday in November with a large feast of turkey with stuffing, sweet potatoes, cranberry sauce, and pumpkin pie for dessert. When the Pilgrims, seeking religious freedom, first came to American shores from England, they endured many hardships. Native Americans taught them how to survive. As a token of gratitude, the Pilgrims invited their Native American friends to share a feast with them. This was the first Thanksgiving and was celebrated in 1621, a year after the arrival of the Pilgrims to Plymouth Rock, in Massachusetts.

A: That turkey sure smells good! When's dinner?

B: Be patient. Aunt Sally is due to arrive any minute with the salad and pumpkin pies, and Uncle Ned'll be here real soon with the refreshments.

A: I can hardly wait!

B: Just take it easy and remember don't let your eyes be bigger than your stomach. Remember how you felt last year when you overate?

A: No problem. This year I have a bigger stomach.

American Superstitions

Friday the Thirteenth

It is believed that the combination of Friday, an unlucky day, and thirteen, an unlucky number, will bring great misfortune.

A: Why are you so late? If we don't go soon, we'll miss our palne.

B: I don't like to tell you this, but we can't leave on our trip today.

A: Why not?

B: I went to pay for the tickets and my wallet was gone. All our money for the trip is lost.

A: I should have known something would happen. Never begin a trip on Friday the thirteenth.

* 자료 : 《101 American Customs》 《101 American Superstitions》에서 발췌

해　석

Chapter 1. 출발에서 도착까지

1. 탑승 전까지의 전반적인 사항들

(1) 항공권 이용에 대한 전반적인 회화

1) 비자 신청(A)

E: 무엇을 도와드릴까요?
T: 비자를 신청하고 싶습니다.
E: 몇 가지 질문에 대답해 주시겠습니까?
T: 물론입니다.
E: 언제 어디서 태어나셨습니까?
T: 1970년 1월 10일에 서울에서 태어났습니다.
E: 비자를 발급받으려는 목적은 무엇입니까?
T: 뉴욕으로 여행을 가기 위해서입니다.
E: 뉴욕에서 얼마 동안 머물 예정입니까?
T: 약 한 달 정도입니다.
E: 이 양식에 기입해주시고, 사진과 함께 제출해주십시오. 그리고 금요일 10시 이후에 언제라도 비자를 찾으러 오십시오.
T: 예, 감사합니다.

2) 비자 신청(B)

T: 미국 비자를 연장하고 싶습니다.
E: 왜 연장하기를 원하십니까?
T: 워싱턴에 있는 대학의 리서치에 참가하기 위해서입니다.
E: 얼마 동안 있을 예정입니까?
T: 6주 동안 있을 겁니다.
E: 비자가 승인되었습니다. 10년 동안 유효합니다.
T: 감사합니다.

3) 항공편 예약(A)

A: 아메리칸 에어라인입니다. 무엇을 도와드릴까요?
T: 예, 저는 인솔자입니다. 뉴욕행 비행기 30좌석을 예약하고 싶습니다.
A: 왕복권 또는 편도권, 어느 것을 원하십니까?
T: 왕복권입니다.

A: 언제 출발하시길 원하십니까?
T: 다음주 월요일입니다. 그날 저녁 비행편이 있습니까?
A: 잠시만 기다려주십시오. 빈 좌석이 있나 한번 확인해 보겠습니다. (잠시 후) 여기에 있습니다.
T: 아, 좋습니다.
A: 오후 6:30, 9:00, 그리고 11:00 이렇게 3번의 비행이 있습니다. 어느 시간을 예약하시길 원하십니까?
T: 오후 6:30 비행편을 예약해주십시오. 요금은 얼마입니까?
A: 어떤 등급을 원하십니까?
T: 일반석을 주십시오.
A: 예, 왕복에 700달러입니다. 성함과 전화번호를 알려 주시겠습니까?
T: 이름은 김입니다. 전화번호는 02-565-6482입니다.
A: 예. 다음주 월요일 오후 6:30 뉴욕행 비행기 AA 210이 예약되었습니다. 비행시간에 변경이 있으시면 연락주십시오.
T: 예. 비행기표는 언제 어디서 살 수 있습니까?
E: 편하실 때 언제든지 공항의 아메리칸 에어라인 창구로 오시면 됩니다.
T: 좋습니다. 신용카드로 구매해도 됩니까?
E: 물론입니다. 모든 신용카드를 다 사용하실 수 있습니다.
T: 잘 되었군요. 감사합니다.
E: 예약해주셔서 감사합니다.

4) 항공편 예약(B)

A: 아메리칸 에어라인의 수입니다. 무엇을 도와드릴까요?
T: 라스베이거스행 좌석이 있습니까?
A: 예, 있습니다.
T: 직항입니까?
A: 아니오, 도쿄를 경유해서 갑니다.
T: 라스베이거스행 비행기는 얼마나 자주 운항하나요?
A: 오전 8시부터 4편이 운항됩니다. 몇 시로 예약해드릴까요?
T: 오후 5시 비행이 좋겠네요.
A: 좌석은 어떻게 드릴까요?
T: 비즈니스석을 왕복으로 예약해주세요.
A: 알겠습니다. 아메리칸 에어라인을 이용해주셔서 감사합니다.

5) 항공편 예약(C)

A: 아메리칸 에어라인입니다. 무엇을 도와드릴까요?
T: 샌프란시스코행 직행편이 있습니까?
A: 예, 있습니다.
T: 얼마나 자주 운항하나요?
A: 오전 6시부터 오전 12시까지 3시간마다 있습니다. 몇 시로 해드릴까요?

T: 3월 12일로 예약해주세요.
A: 죄송하지만 그날은 빈 좌석이 없네요. 돌아오실 날은 언제인가요?
T: 3월 19일이에요.
A: 3월 13일 오후 9시 비행편만 남아 있습니다.
T: 너무 늦는데요. 3월 12일 대기자명단에 올려주시겠어요.
A: 예, 알겠습니다. 만약 12일에 취소된 좌석이 있다면 연락드리겠습니다.
T: 좋습니다. 감사합니다.

6) 항공편 예약(D)

T: 하와이행 밤 비행편은 몇 시에 있나요?
A: 오후 8시에 떠납니다.
T: 몇 시간 걸리나요?
A: 5시간 걸립니다.
T: 일반석 왕복요금은 어떻게 되나요?
A: 420달러입니다, 손님.
T: 좀더 싼 표는 없을까요?
A: 있습니다. 그러나 괌을 경유해서 하와이로 가는 비행편이고, 시간은 10시간 걸립니다.
T: 좋습니다, 그것으로 하겠어요.

7) 항공편 예약(E)

A: 안녕하세요, 아메리칸 에어라인에 전화주셔서 감사합니다. 무엇을 도와드릴까요?
T: 예, 1월 25일 일요일 오전 뉴욕으로 가는 비행편을 예약하고 싶은데요. 좌석이 있을까요?
A: 예, 있습니다. 오전 11시와 오후 8시 두 번 운항합니다.
T: 직항인가요?
A: 아니오, 앵커리지에서 1시간 정도 머뭅니다.
T: 한 시간 정도는 나쁘지 않군요.
A: 예, 오전에는 뉴욕에 도착하실 수 있습니다.
T: 좋습니다. 오전 11시 비행기로 일반석 예약하고 싶은데, 빈 좌석이 있나요?
A: 예, 있습니다. 한번 확인해 보겠습니다.
T: 네, 부탁합니다.
A: 일반석에 빈자리가 있네요.
T: 뉴욕까지 가는 일반석의 요금은 얼마인가요?
A: 505달러입니다.
T: 일반석과 일등석의 요금차이는 어떻게 되나요?
A: 일등석은 720달러입니다.
T: 예, 일반석으로 예약해주세요. 11시 비행기는 어느 공항에서 떠나나요?
A: LA 국제공항입니다.
T: 공항에서 비행기표를 받을 수 있나요?

A: 예, 그러나 적어도 출발시간 1시간 전에는 나오셔야 합니다.

(2) 탑승편의 재확인

1) 전화로 탑승편 확인(A)

A: 아메리칸 에어라인입니다. 무엇을 도와드릴까요?

T: 예약을 확인하고 싶습니다.

A: 성함과 비행편 번호를 말씀해주십시오.

T: 이름은 김이며, 비행편 번호는 다음주 월요일 뉴욕행 AA 210입니다.

A: 잠시만 기다리십시오. 확인해보겠습니다. 손님의 일반석 예약이 확인되었습니다.

T: 예. 공항에 몇 시까지 가야 합니까?

A: 탑승시간 두 시간 전에는 공항에 도착하셔야 합니다. 그리고 보딩 시간은 오후 6시입니다.

T: 휴대물은 몇 개까지 가능합니까?

A: 좌석 밑에 둘 수 있을 정도 크기의 수하물 한 개만 허용합니다.

T: 알겠습니다. 감사합니다.

2) 전화로 탑승편 확인(B)

A: 아메리칸 에어라인 그룹 데스크입니다.

T: 우리 그룹 30명에 대한 좌석을 재확인하고 싶습니다.

A: 그룹명이 어떻게 되나요?

T: 해피 투어입니다.

A: 잠시만 기다리세요. 예, 이번주 수요일 저녁 필라델피아행 271 비행편에 30명분의 좌석이 예약확인 되었습니다. 성함과 전화번호를 알려주시겠어요?

T: 숙소는 리츠 호텔이고, 전화번호는 714-576-2878이며, 이름은 김입니다.

A: 알겠습니다. 오후 6시까지 공항으로 오셔야 합니다.

3) 전화로 탑승편 확인(C)

A: 아메리칸 에어라인의 메리입니다. 무엇을 도와드릴까요?

T: 예약을 재확인하고 싶은데요.

A: 성함과 비행편을 말씀해주세요.

T: 이름은 김이고, 비행편은 273편입니다.

A: 목요일 오후 1시 30분에 런던으로 떠나는 비행편 맞나요?

T: 맞습니다.

A: 잠시만 기다리세요. 예약이 재확인되었습니다.

T: 감사합니다.

4) 전화로 탑승편 확인(D)

T: 제 이름은 김이고, 내일 오후 시카고행 807 비행편의 예약을 재확인하고 싶습니다.

A: 잠시만 기다리세요. 미스터 김. 뉴욕에서 예약하셨나요?

T: 예, 그렇습니다.
A: 좋습니다. 확인전화 주셔서 감사합니다. 또 뭐 도와드릴 것은 없나요?
T: 예, 그 비행편을 위해 비행장까지 가는 공항버스가 있나요?
A: 예, 있습니다. 비행기 출발 세 시간 전에 중앙 버스터미널에서 떠납니다.
T: 감사합니다. 그리고 국제선의 경우 일등석의 수하물 제약은 얼마인가요?
A: 25kg입니다. 작은 크기의 여행가방 하나는 기내로 가지고 타셔서 좌석 밑에 놓으시면 됩니다.
T: 알겠습니다, 감사합니다.
A: 아메리칸 에어라인을 이용해주셔서 감사합니다.

5) 전화로 탑승편을 확인했는데 다른 단체의 이름으로 예약되어 있을 경우

T: 안녕하세요. 아메리칸 에어라인 티켓 카운터입니까?
A: 예, 무엇을 도와드릴까요?
T: 다음주 월요일 오전에 뉴욕으로 떠나는 비행편 예약을 재확인하고 싶습니다. 뉴욕행 아메리칸 에어라인 210편에 탑승합니다. 우리팀 30명 모두에 대한 예약을 재확인하고 싶습니다. 확인해 주시겠습니까?
A: 예, 항공권 발행 때 예약을 하셨습니까?
T: 예, 서울에서 했습니다.
A: 단체명을 알려주십시오.
T: 해피 투어입니다.
A: 잠시만 기다리십시오. 제가 예약을 확인해 보겠습니다. 음.. 죄송하지만 손님의 단체명은 예약 리스트에 없습니다.
T: 경민 문화관광산업연구소로 되어 있을 겁니다. 다시 한번 주의 깊게 확인해 주시겠습니까?
A: 잠시만 기다리십시오. 아! 여기에 있군요. 손님의 단체는 다음주 월요일에 아메리칸 에어라인 210편을 타고 뉴욕으로 떠나게 되어 있지요?
T: 예, 그렇습니다.
A: 30명의 좌석이 예약되어 있습니다. 연락처 좀 알려 주시겠습니까?
T: 한국대학이고요, 전화번호는 02-595-7228입니다. 제 이름은 김입니다.
A: 예, 알겠습니다. 탑승할 비행기는 오전 11시에 출발하기로 되어 있습니다.
T: 몇 시까지 공항에서 체크인을 해야 합니까?
A: 늦어도 9시까지는 하셔야 합니다.
T: 저, 그런데 기내식은 나옵니까?
A: 예, 저녁과 아침이 나옵니다.
T: 미리 메뉴를 알 수 있을까요?
A: 죄송하지만 지금은 정확히 알 수가 없습니다. 괜찮으시면 제가 나중에 전화로 알려드려도 될까요?
T: 예, 도와주셔서 감사합니다.
A: 천만에 말씀이십니다.
T: 감사합니다. 안녕히 계십시오.

(3) 항공편 예약 변경

A: 안녕하십니까, 아메리칸 에어라인입니다. 무엇을 도와드릴까요?
T: 예약을 변경하고 싶습니다.
A: 성함과 비행편 번호를 알려주십시오.
T: 이름은 김이며, 비행편 번호는 이번주 목요일 뉴욕행 AA 210입니다.
A: 잠시만 기다리십시오. 어떻게 변경하시길 원하십니까?
T: 이번주 토요일에 시카고로 출발하는 비행편으로 변경하고 싶습니다.
A: 예, 알겠습니다. 이번주 토요일 오후 8시 시카고행 AA 710이 있습니다. 괜찮으시겠습니까?
T: 예, 그것으로 하겠습니다.
A: 변경되었습니다.
T: 감사합니다.
A: 천만에 말씀이십니다. 좋은 하루 되십시오.

(4) 항공편 예약 취소

A: 아메리칸 에어라인입니다. 무엇을 도와드릴까요?
T: 이번주 일요일에 뉴욕으로 가는 비행편 예약을 취소하고 싶습니다.
A: 성함을 말씀해주십시오.
T: 김입니다.
A: 다른 변경사항은 없습니까?
T: 아니오, 없습니다. 감사합니다.

(5) 항공 티켓 구매

A: 안녕하세요, 무엇을 도와드릴까요?
T: 티켓을 구매하고 싶습니다.
A: 예약은 하셨습니까?
T: 물론입니다. 이미 예약을 했습니다.
A: 알겠습니다. 성함과 비행편을 알려주십시오.
T: 김이고, AA 210입니다.
A: 예, 미스터 김. 뉴욕으로 떠나는 210편 일반석이 예약이 되어 있습니다. 왕복요금은 700달러입니다. 돌아오는 항공편을 예약해드릴까요?
T: 예, 8월 31일 비행편으로 예약을 원합니다.
A: 어떻게 지불하시겠습니까?
T: 마스터 카드도 됩니까?
A: 물론입니다. 신용카드와 ID 카드를 주시겠습니까?
T: 여기 있습니다.
A: 잠시만 기다리십시오. 곧 오겠습니다. 기다려주셔서 감사합니다. 미스터 김.

여기에 사인을 해주시고, 전화번호를 적어주십시오.
T: 예, 여기 있습니다.
A: 손님의 표는 8월 25일 뉴욕으로 출발하는 210편 일반석입니다. 짐은 있으십니까?
T: 예, 가방이 하나 있습니다.
A: 만약 원하신다면 운반인이 손님의 짐 수속을 도와줄 수 있습니다.
T: 좋습니다.
A: 여기 표가 있습니다. 출입구는 21번입니다.
T: 감사합니다.

(6) 항공사 카운터에서

1) 체크인(A)

A: 안녕하세요, 무엇을 도와드릴까요?
T: 예, 체크인을 하고 싶습니다.
A: 성함이 어떻게 되십니까?
T: 해피 투어의 김입니다.
A: 예, 손님은 예약이 되어 있습니다. 비행기표와 여권을 보여 주시겠습니까?
T: 여기 있습니다.
A: 흡연석과 금연석 어디를 원하십니까?
T: 금연석으로 주십시오. 그리고 좌석 5개는 복도 쪽으로 원합니다.
A: 짐은 있으십니까?
T: 여행용 가방이 30개 있습니다.
A: 원하신다면 여기서 짐을 부쳐 드리겠습니다.
T: 예, 좋습니다.
A: 여기에 올려 주시겠습니까?
T: 예.
A: 감사합니다. 손님의 좌석번호는 18H에서 27C까지입니다. 여권, 표, 탑승권, 수하물표 있습니다. 좋은 비행 되십시오.
T: 감사합니다.

2) 체크인(B)

T: 보스턴행 아메리칸 에어라인 587편 체크인을 여기서 하나요?
A: 티켓을 받으셨나요?
T: 예, 여기 있습니다.
A: 감사합니다. 짐을 여기에 올려주시겠어요?
T: 예, 전 여행가방 하나만 있습니다.
A: 보스턴행 587편 일등석 맞지요?
T: 예.
A: 창가 쪽을 드릴까요, 복도 쪽을 드릴까요?

T: 복도 쪽을 주세요.
A: 좌석은 18C입니다. 표와 여권 그리고 보딩 패스 여기 있습니다.
T: 몇 시에 출발하나요?
A: 오전 11시에 출발합니다.
T: 지금 어디로 가야 하나요?
A: 세관과 이민국으로 가세요.
T: 감사합니다.

(7) 수화물

1) 중량 초과시(A)

T: 여기서 이 비행기 체크인을 합니까?
A: 예, 그렇습니다. 여권과 표를 보여주십시오.
T: 여기에 있습니다.
A: 짐을 여기에 올려주십시오.
T: 예.
A: 짐이 중량 초과입니다.
T: 추가요금은 얼마입니까?
A: 25달러입니다.
T: 알겠습니다. 여기 있습니다.
A: 표와 탑승권입니다. 좋은 여행 되십시오.

2) 중량 초과시(B)

A: 짐 있으세요?
T: 예, 여행가방 세 개 있어요.
A: 두 개만 허용되고, 나머지는 추가요금을 지불하셔야 합니다.
T: 추가요금은 얼마지요?
A: 1킬로그램당 10달러입니다.
T: 이 가방들을 모두 가져갈 수 없나요?
A: 죄송하지만 가방이 커서 좌석 밑에 들어가지 않습니다.
T: 좋습니다. 탑승시간은 언제지요?
A: 오후 2시 30분입니다.
T: 입구는 몇 번인가요?
A: 16번입니다.

(8) 보안 검색대

1) 보안 검색대를 지날 때(A)

S: 모든 짐을 운반대 위에 올려 주시겠습니까? 이쪽으로 서십시오. 주머니는 모두 비우시고, 지나가십시오.

T: 이 디지털 카메라는 어떻게 해야 합니까?
S: 저에게 주십시오. 이것은 검색장치를 통과할 필요가 없습니다.
T: 예.
S: 가방을 열어봐도 되겠습니까?
T: 물론입니다. 여기 있습니다.
S: CD 플레이어를 꺼주시겠습니까?
T: 오, 미안합니다.
S: 괜찮습니다. 협조해주셔서 감사합니다.

2) 보안 검색대를 지날 때(B)

(삐)
S: 이쪽으로 서주세요. 주머니에 뭐가 있나요?
T: 오, 죄송합니다. 동전 몇 개에요.
S: 좋습니다. 감사합니다. 보안대에 가져온 짐을 모두 올려주세요. 이 가방을 열어봐도 되겠습니까?
T: 예, 열어보세요. 여기 있습니다.

2. 기내에서의 각종 회화

(1) 기내에서 좌석을 찾을 때

1) 기내에서 좌석을 찾을 때 사용되는 회화(A)

A: 안녕하세요, 어서 오십시오. 보딩 패스를 보여주시겠습니까?
T: 여기 있습니다.
A: 감사합니다. 손님의 좌석은 28C입니다. 손님 왼쪽에 있는 승무원실 뒤쪽에 있습니다. 가방을 들어드릴까요?
T: 아니오, 괜찮습니다. 가방은 어디에 두어야 합니까?
A: 손님 앞좌석 밑이나, 머리 위 선반에 두시면 됩니다. 무거운 짐은 좌석 밑에다 두십시오.
T: 그렇게 하겠습니다.

2) 기내에서 좌석을 찾을 때 사용되는 회화(B)

T: 제 좌석이 어딘가요?
A: 탑승권을 좀 보여주시겠어요.
T: 여기 있습니다.
A: 감사합니다. 좌석은 26K입니다. 곧장 밑으로 12줄 정도 가시면 됩니다.
T: 감사합니다. 혹시 빈 좌석이 있나요?
A: 예, 그러나 이륙하기 전까지는 기다리셔야 합니다.
T: 좋습니다. 좌석에 기대도 됩니까?
A: 아직 안 됩니다. 이륙하기 전까지 기다리세요.

3) 기내에서 좌석을 찾을 때 사용되는 회화(C)

T: 가방 어디에다 둬야 하나요?
A: 손님 앞 좌석 밑에 넣으시거나 머리 위 선반에 넣으세요.
T: 화장실은 어디 있나요?
A: 비행기 뒤쪽에 4개의 화장실이 있습니다.
T: 이륙할 준비가 다 되었나요?
A: 예, 좌석에 앉으셔서 안전벨트를 매세요.
T: 알겠습니다.

4) 기내에서 좌석을 찾을 때 사용되는 회화(D)

A: 탑승권 좀 보여주세요.
T: 여기 있습니다. 10G라고 되어 있네요.
A: 왼쪽편의 첫번째 구역 통로 쪽입니다.
T: 감사합니다. 이 가방은 어디다 둬야 하나요?
A: 좌석 위 보관선반에 올려놓으세요. 그리고 도착 전에 좀 쉬고 싶으시면 베개도 담요와 그곳에 있으니 사용하시면 됩니다.
T: 필요할 거 같군요. 이륙하려면 얼마나 더 있어야 하나요?
A: 10분 안에 출발할 겁니다. 원하시면 잡지 몇 권을 가져다 드릴까요?
T: 감사합니다.
A: 이륙 후에 가져다 드리겠습니다. 또한 음료수도 제공해 드리겠습니다.

(2) 단체여행 때 기내에 들어가서 바로 사용하는 회화

A: 안녕하십니까?
T: 안녕하세요. 우리는 모두 30명입니다. 우리의 자리가 어디인지 알 수 있습니까? 우리 중의 네 명은 금연석입니다.
A: 탑승권 좀 보여주시겠습니까?
T: 예, 여기 있습니다.
A: 좌석은 27A에서 30H입니다. 왼쪽으로 두번째 구역입니다. 금연석은 1A에서 B, C, D입니다.
T: 예, 대단히 감사합니다.
A: 기내로 가지고 들어오신 수하물은 머리 위 선반이 아닌 좌석 아래쪽에 두도록 사람들에게 전해주십시오.
T: 우리는 작은 가방 하나밖에 없습니다. 이것을 어디에 두어야 하지요?
A: 기내 물건 보관함에 두겠습니다. 그런데, 손님은 해피 투어 그룹의 TC입니까? 제 이름은 엔야입니다.
T: 반갑습니다, 엔야씨. 전 이 그룹의 인솔자이고, 이름은 김입니다.
A: 어디까지 가십니까?
T: 뉴욕까지 갑니다. 우리 팀들이 식사 주문시 도움이 될 수 있도록 메뉴를 좀 볼 수 있습니까?

A: 참 친절하시네요, 김
T: 어떤 종류의 음료수가 있나요?
A: 알코올 음료와 비알코올 음료를 제공하고 있습니다.
T: 카페인 없는 커피는 있습니까?
A: 죄송합니다. 저희 비행기에는 카페인 없는 커피는 없습니다.
T: 예. 알겠습니다. 저녁식사는 몇 시에 제공됩니까?
A: 5시에 제공됩니다.
T: 예. 우리 팀원들에게 뭐 읽을거리 좀 가져다주실 수 있으십니까?
A: 물론입니다.
T: 감사합니다. 그리고, 담요도 좀 필요합니다. 여분의 담요가 있나요?
A: 예, 머리 위 선반에 몇 개 있습니다.
T: 예, 오늘 기내 영화상영은 있습니까?
A: 예. 하나 있습니다.
T: 어떤 영화지요?
A: "나쁜 녀석들 2"입니다.
T: 좋습니다. 감사합니다.
A: 천만에요. 즐거운 시간 되십시오.

(3) 좌석 변경시

1) 좌석을 변경하고 싶을 때(A)

T: 실례합니다만 좌석을 교환할 수 있을까요?
A: 좌석에 무슨 문제라도 있으십니까?
T: 우리 일원 중 한 명이 고소공포증이 있어서 창 밖의 광경을 무서워합니다.
A: 좌석이 있는지 한번 살펴보겠습니다. 모든 분들이 다 탑승하신 후에 다시 와서 빈 좌석의 여부를 알려 드리겠습니다.
T: 감사합니다.
A: (잠시 후) 기다려주셔서 감사합니다. 끝 줄에 빈 좌석이 몇 개 있습니다. 그쪽은 괜찮으시겠습니까?
T: 물론입니다. 좋습니다.
A: 이쪽으로 오십시오. 여기입니다.
T: 너무 감사합니다.
A: 천만에요. 좋은 비행 되십시오.

2) 좌석을 변경하고 싶을 때(B)

T: 좌석을 변경할 수 있을까요? 만약 가능하다면 너무 감사하겠어요.
A: 이 좌석에 무슨 문제가 있으세요?
T: 전 담배연기를 무척 싫어해서 금역구역으로 옮기고 싶습니다.
A: 잠시만 기다리세요. 예, 금연구역에 좌석이 많이 비어 있군요. 이리로 오세요.
T: 너무 감사합니다.

(4) 이륙할 때

A: 손님, 좌석 벨트를 매주시고, 좌석을 똑바로 펴주십시오.
T: 어떻게 하는지를 잘 모르겠는데요.
A: 이 벨트를 이렇게 당기고 이것을 매면 됩니다.
T: 감사합니다. 아, 좌석이 고장인 것 같습니다. 뒤로 젖힐 수가 없네요.
A: 이것을 누르면 이렇게 됩니다. 됐지요?
T: 아, 알겠습니다. 그리고 토하고 싶은데요, 멀미약과 위생대를 좀 주시겠습니까?
A: 잠시만 기다리세요. 곧 약을 가져다 드리겠습니다. 요즘에 비행기 여행은 매우 편안합니다. 날씨가 나쁘지 않다면 비행기는 어떤 진동도 느껴지지 않습니다.
T: 알겠습니다.

(5) 음료 서비스

1) 음료 서비스를 받을 때(A)

T: 실례합니다. 우리 일원들이 음료수를 원하는데, 서비스해주실 수 있으십니까?
A: 무엇을 드시겠습니까. 손님?
T: 청량 음료수는 있습니까?
A: 물론입니다. 7업, 콜라, 오렌지 주스, 토마토 주스, 파인애플 주스, 그리고 망고 주스가 있습니다. 어떤 음료를 원하십니까?
T: 얼음을 가득 채운 콜라 5잔, 망고 주스 12잔, 세븐업 13잔을 주십시오.
A: 예, 알겠습니다. 곧 가지고 오겠습니다.

2) 음료 서비스를 받을 때(B)

T: 실례하지만 음료수 좀 주실래요?
A: 어떤 것으로 드릴까요?
T: 진토닉 있나요?
A: 예, 있습니다. 잠시만 기다리세요. 제가 곧 가져다 드리겠습니다.

3) 음료 서비스를 받을 때(C)

A: 무엇을 드시겠어요?
T: 무슨 종류가 있나요?
A: 오렌지 주스, 토마토 주스, 홍차, 커피와 콜라가 있습니다.
T: 레몬을 넣은 홍차를 주시겠어요?
A: 여기 있습니다, 손님.
T: 감사합니다. 얼마인가요?
A: 홍차, 커피와 콜라는 무료입니다.

(6) 식사 서비스

1) 식사 서비스를 받을 때(A)

A: 좌석을 똑바로 펴주십시오. 곧 음식을 제공할 예정입니다. 테이블을 앞으로 빼주시겠습니까, 손님?

T: 예.

A: 닭고기와 소고기 중 어느 것을 드시겠습니까?

T: 생선은 없나요? 우리 중 한 명이 채식주의자입니다.

A: 죄송하지만 생선은 없습니다. 하지만 괜찮으시다면 해산물 스파게티를 제공해 드릴 수 있습니다.

T: 좋습니다. 그것으로 하겠습니다. 그리고 나머지는 닭고기 9개와 소고기 20개로 하겠습니다.

A: 포도주 드시겠습니까? 백포도주와 적포도주가 있습니다.

T: 백포도주 5잔과 적포도주 15잔 주십시오. 우리 중 몇 명은 술을 못합니다. 그들에게 음료수를 가져다 주시겠습니까?

A: 예, 그렇게 하겠습니다. 여기 있습니다. 즐거운 식사 되십시오.

T: 감사합니다.

2) 식사 서비스를 받을 때(B)

A: 점심하시겠어요?

T: 예.

A: 세 가지 종류가 있는데요. 전통 미국식 소고기 스테이크, 한국식 불고기 백반과 중국식 자장면이 있습니다. 어떤 것을 드시겠어요?

T: 중국식으로 주세요.

A: 와인이나 칵테일 하시겠어요? 와인은 백포도주와 적포도주가 있습니다.

T: 백포도주를 주세요.

A: 여기 있습니다. 다른 것은 필요없으세요?

T: 없습니다. 충분합니다.

A: 맛있게 드세요.

3) 식사 서비스를 받을 때(C)

A: 무엇을 도와드릴까요?

T: 질문 하나 해도 됩니까?

A: 예, 하세요.

T: 저녁식사는 언제 제공되나요? 굶어죽기 직전이에요.

A: 저녁식사는 6시에 제공됩니다.

T: 지금 5시군요. 1시간만 기다리면 되겠네요.

A: 죄송하지만 2시간 기다리셔야 됩니다. 동부시간으로 사용하거든요.

T: 아, 알겠어요.

A: 대신에 음료수라도 드릴게요.

T: 감사합니다.

(7) 기내 서비스

1) 담요와 기내 영화 서비스(A)

T: 담요를 주시겠습니까?
A: 예, 여기 있습니다.
T: 감사합니다. 이 전등은 어떻게 끄나요?
A: 여기 이 버튼을 누르시면 됩니다. 그리고 팔을 내리시고, 편한 휴식을 취하실 수 있습니다.
T: 고맙습니다. 기내에서 영화 상영은 합니까?
A: 오늘 "슈렉"이라는 애니메이션 영화를 상영합니다.
T: 아, 그 영화 좋아합니다.
A: 이어폰을 가져다 드리겠습니다. 입체음향을 느끼실 수 있을 겁니다.
T: 좋습니다. 영화 소리는 몇 번 채널에서 들을 수 있습니까?
A: 영어는 2번 채널이고, 한국어는 1번 채널입니다.

2) 담요와 기내 영화 서비스(B)

T: 낮잠을 자고 싶은데, 담요와 베개 좀 주시겠어요?
A: 잠시만 기다리세요. 여기에 있습니다.
T: 감사합니다. 그리고 이어폰도 주시겠어요?
A: 영화를 보시려고 하나요?
T: 아니오, 음악을 들으려고 합니다.
A: 예, 이어폰을 가져다 드리겠습니다. 스테레오 음악을 즐기실 수 있을 겁니다.
T: 음악 채널이 어떻게 되나요?
A: 3번부터 14번까지 있습니다. 3번부터 6번은 한국음악, 7번부터 11번은 미국음악, 12번은 일본음악, 13번은 중국음악, 14번은 유럽음악입니다.
T: 너무 감사합니다.

3) 담요와 기내 영화 서비스(C)

T: 우리는 30명인 단체입니다.
A: 아, 인솔자인가요?
T: 예, 만약 여유분이 있다면 담요 몇 장 더 주시겠어요?
A: 물론입니다. 머리 위 선반에 있습니다.
T: 감사합니다.
(잠시 후)
T: 실례합니다만 일원 중 한 명이 속이 안 좋다고 합니다. 혹시 소화제 있나요?
A: 예, 곧 가져다 드리겠습니다.
T: 감사합니다. 그리고 종이봉지도 좀 필요합니다.
A: 여기에 있습니다.
(잠시 후) 괜찮으세요?
T: 예, 한결 나아진 거 같습니다.

(8) 도착시간 문의

T: 실례합니다만 뉴욕에는 몇 시에 도착합니까?
A: 잠시만요. 현지 시간으로 오전 11시에 도착합니다.
T: 알겠습니다. 서울과 뉴욕간의 비행시간은 얼마나 되지요?
A: 약 11시간 정도 됩니다.
T: 서울과 뉴욕간의 시차는 어떻게 되지요?
A: 13시간입니다. 서울이 13시간 빠릅니다.
T: 미국으로 가는 데에는 하루가 빠릅니까, 아니면 하루가 늦습니까?
A: 하루가 늦습니다. 그래서 우리는 같은 날에 도착하게 되는 겁니다.
T: 예, 그렇군요.

(9) 입국 신고서 및 세관 신고서 기재

A: 입국 신고서를 써주십시오
T: 좀 도와 주시겠습니까?
A: 예, 무엇을 도와드릴까요?
T: 세관 신고서를 다 작성하였는데 모두 정확한가요?
A: 귀중품이나 10,000달러 이상 있으시면 모두 신고해야 합니다.
T: 예, 알겠습니다.
A: 그리고 여기에 손님의 여권번호와 비자번호를 기입해주십시오.
T: 도와주셔서 감사합니다. 모두 다 맞나요?
A: 예, 정확합니다. 손님.

(10) 착륙할 때

A: 실례합니다만 손님, 좌석 벨트를 매주십시오. 곧 착륙할 예정입니다.
T: 알겠습니다.
A: 비행기가 완전히 멈출 때까지 좌석에서 일어나지 마십시오.
T: 드디어 시카고에 도착했네요. 천천히 착륙중인 것 같군요. 그렇지요?
A: 예, 그렇습니다. 즐거운 비행이 되었기를 희망합니다.
T: 예, 즐거운 비행이었습니다. 그리고 좋은 서비스에 감사합니다.
A: 아닙니다. 제 임무였을 뿐인걸요. 마지막 목적지가 어디입니까?
T: 뉴욕입니다. 케네디 공항에서 내려야 합니다.
A: 지금 인사를 드려야겠습니다. 안녕히 가십시오. 그리고 다시 뵙기를 희망합니다.
T: 그러지요. 감사합니다.

3. 검역과 통관수속

(1) 검역에서의 회화

O: 예방접종 증명서를 보여주세요.
T: 여기 있습니다.
O: SARS 예방접종은 하셨습니까?
T: SARS 예방접종은 하지 않았습니다. 저희들은 한국에서 왔습니다.
O: 예, 알겠습니다. 괜찮습니다. 입국관리 쪽으로 가주세요.

(2) 입국수속 회화

T: 안녕하십니까?
O: 안녕하십니까? 여권 좀 보여주시겠습니까?
T: 여기 있습니다.
O: 어디서 왔습니까?
T: 한국에서 왔습니다.
O: 당신은 인솔자입니까?
T: 그렇습니다.
O: 모두 몇 명입니까?
T: 저까지 포함해서 30명입니다.
O: 이번 여행의 목적은 무엇입니까? 사업차 오셨습니까? 아니면 관광차 오셨습니까?
T: 관광차 왔습니다.
O: 얼마나 오랫동안 미국에서 체류할 겁니까?
T: 한 달 정도 머물 예정입니다.
O: 어디에서 숙박합니까?
T: 뉴욕에서는 힐튼 호텔에서 머뭅니다.
O: 어딜 여행합니까?
T: 뉴욕에서 10일, 그리고 보스턴, 시카고, 라스베이거스로 갑니다.
O: 꽤 괜찮은 여행입니다. 여기 여권이 있습니다.
T: 감사합니다.
O: 미국에 오신 것을 환영합니다. 좋은 여행 되십시오.
T: 감사합니다.

(3) 세관심사 회화

O: 안녕하세요, 신고하실 거 있으십니까?
T: 아니오. 없습니다. 우리 일행은 모두 30명이며, 저는 인솔자입니다. 우리는 모두 30개의 가방뿐입니다.

O: 술이나, 담배, 진주 같은 것은 없습니까?
T: 각자 위스키 두 병, 담배 100 이외에 귀금속과 보석은 가지고 있지 않습니다.
O: 식물이나 동물은 있습니까?
T: 아니오, 가지고 있지 않습니다.
O: 좋습니다. 가방을 열어주세요. 이것은 무엇입니까?
T: 미숫가루의 일종으로 내 음식입니다.
O: 저 상자는 무엇입니까?
T: 이것은 내 심장약입니다.
O: 종이로 포장된 것은 무엇입니까?
T: 마른오징어입니다.
O: 그리고 이것은 무엇입니까?
T: 이것은 라면입니다.
O: 예, 좋습니다. 협조해주셔서 감사합니다.
T: 천만에 말씀입니다.
O: 좋은 여행 되십시오.
T: 감사합니다.

(4) 짐 분실시

T: 실례합니다만, 제 짐이 아직 도착하지 않았습니다.
A: 진정하십시오, 손님. 비행편 명이 어떻게 됩니까?
T: 음, 서울로부터 온 아메리칸 에어라인입니다.
A: AA 210편이지요?
T: 예, 모든 사람들의 짐은 다 나왔고, 수하물 컨테이너도 멈췄지만 아직 제 짐은 나오지 않았습니다.
A: 오, 죄송합니다. 손님의 짐에 이름과 주소를 적어두셨습니까?
T: 물론입니다. 이름, 주소, 우편번호, 핸드폰 전화번호까지 다 기입했습니다.
A: 저희가 손님의 짐을 최대한 빨리 찾아보겠습니다. 이 서류에 기입을 해주시겠습니까? 그리고 손님의 짐과 비행편 명, 물건들의 가치 등도 상세히 기입해주십시오.
T: 알겠습니다.
A: 물건 품목을 정리한 목록을 가지고 있습니까?
T: 아니오, 왜 그럽니까?
A: 보험회사에서 목록에 대해 요청할 것입니다. 적어두시는 것이 나을 것입니다.
T: 알겠습니다. 약간 긴장이 되는군요. 저의 친구도 지난달 짐을 잃어버렸는데, 아직도 찾지 못했습니다.
A: 걱정하지 마시고, 마음을 편안히 하십시오. 잃어버린 수하물의 대부분은 다시 찾을 수 있습니다.
T: 그러길 바랍니다.
A: 만약 12시간 안에 짐을 되찾지 못한다면 보험회사에서 손님이 당장 필요로

하시는 깨끗한 셔츠나 양말, 속옷 같은 필수품을 살 수 있도록 지원할 것입니다.

T: 알겠습니다.

4. 포터와의 회화

(1) 환승버스에 탈 때 수화물 관리와 포터와의 대화

T: 안녕하세요, 이 수화물을 옮겨서 해피 투어사의 버스에 실어주세요.
P: 예, 전부 몇 개입니까?
T: 30개입니다. 전부 눈에 띄게 하기 위해서 해피 투어사의 흰색 짐표가 붙여져 있습니다.
P: 좋습니다. 클레임 태그를 주시겠어요?
T: 여기 있습니다. 몇 개 있습니까?
P: 정확히 다 있습니다.
T: 짐들을 잠시만 보관해주세요. 버스를 찾아보고 곧 돌아오겠습니다.

Chapter 2. 공항에서 호텔까지

1. 미팅 서비스와 짐의 의논

(1) 공항에 도착하였을 때

1) 현지 여행사와 미팅 스태프와의 대화(A)

R: 실례합니다만, 해피 투어에서 오신 미스터 김이십니까?
T: 예, 그렇습니다. 글로벌 여행사 에이전시에서 오신 미스터 이입니까?
R: 예, 만나서 반갑습니다. 뉴욕에 잘 오셨습니다.
T: 예, 저도 만나서 반갑습니다.
R: 여행은 어떠셨습니까?
T: 너무 좋았습니다. 이렇게 마중나와 주셔서 너무 감사합니다.
R: 별 말씀을 다하십니다. 아메리칸 에어라인을 타고 오셨지요?
T: 예, 서비스가 너무 좋았습니다.
R: 다행입니다. 제가 듣기로는 일행이 30명이라고 했는데, 모두 오셨습니까?
T: 예, 저까지 포함해서 30명입니다.
R: 예, 알겠습니다. 이 짐이 모두 다입니까? 다시 한번 확인해주세요.
T: 예, 전부 다입니다. 해피 투어의 흰색 짐표가 붙어 있는 짐이 30개입니다.
R: 예, 우리의 운전사가 여러분들의 짐을 잘 다룰 것입니다. 이쪽으로 오세요.

T: 감사합니다.
R: 어디서 머물 예정이십니까?
T: 힐튼 호텔에서 머물 예정입니다.
R: 힐튼은 뉴욕에서 가장 좋은 호텔 중에 하나입니다. 제가 호텔까지 안내해 드리겠습니다.
T: 예, 감사합니다. 인환증을 받을 수 있겠습니까?
R: 지금은 가지고 있지 않습니다. 버스 안에서 드리겠습니다.
T: 예, 좋습니다. 감사합니다.

2) 현지 여행사와 미팅 스태프와의 대화(B)

T: 아메리칸 여행사에서 오셨나요?
R: 예, 당신이 김이군요. 전 다니엘입니다. 워싱턴에 오신 걸 환영합니다.
T: 감사합니다. 만나서 반갑습니다. 이 가방들을 버스로 옮겨주세요. 그리고, 저까지 포함해서 31명입니다.
R: 알겠습니다. 모두 탑승하셨나요?
T: 예, 그리고 바우처를 확인할 수 있을까요?
R: 물론입니다. 여기에 있습니다. 그리고 여행일정표 31장도 있습니다.
T: 감사합니다.

2. 환승버스의 의논

(1) 현지 여행사의 미팅 스태프와 환승할 버스와의 미팅

T: 버스는 어디에 있습니까?
R: 버스는 공항 뒤쪽에 주차되어 있습니다. 여기서 조금만 걸으면 됩니다. 제가 그곳까지 안내해 드리겠습니다.
T: 예, 지금 버스를 타도 됩니까?
R: 예, 모두 다 탑승하셨습니까?
T: 일행 중 10명이 지금 화장실에 갔으니까 잠시만 기다려주십시오.
R: 알겠습니다.
T: 짐은 모두 다 있습니까?
R: 30개 전부 다 있습니다. 인환증과 30부의 여행일정표를 전해 드리겠습니다.
T: 감사합니다.
R: 인환증은 30장의 쿠폰이 하나로 되어 있습니다. 한번 확인해보십시오.
T: 틀림없습니다.
R: 만약 변경사항이 있을 때에는 뒷면에 자세히 기입해주십시오.
T: 예, 그렇게 하겠습니다. 모두 다 오셨군요. 출발해도 되겠습니다.

3. 리무진버스, 렌터카 등의 이용방법

(1) 수배한 버스가 공항에 안 왔을 경우

P: 당신 버스는 어디에 있습니까?

T: 버스는 와 있을 겁니다. 글로벌 여행사의 버스입니다. 저 파란색 버스가 우리 버스입니까?

P: 아니오. 다른 단체의 버스입니다.

T: 버스회사에 연락해서 어떻게 된 것인지 알아봐야겠습니다. 공중전화는 어디에 있지요?

P: 이쪽으로 곧바로 가면 있습니다. 동전은 가지고 있습니까? 공중전화를 사용하려면 동전이 있어야 합니다.

T: 예, 가지고 있습니다. (전화로) 글로벌 여행사입니까? 배차담당자와 통화하고 싶습니다.

B: 배차담당 지나입니다. 무엇을 도와드릴까요?

T: 저는 한국에서 온 해피 투어의 인솔자입니다. 우리는 지금 공항에서 버스를 기다리고 있는데 버스를 찾을 수가 없군요.

B: 예, 이야기를 계속 하십시오.

T: 버스를 계속 찾아봤는데 찾을 수가 없습니다. 어떻게 된 겁니까?

B: 이렇게 빠른 비행기로 도착할지 몰랐습니다. 귀하의 단체손님은 아메리칸 에어라인 210편으로 오후 2시에 도착하기로 되어 있습니다.

T: 그럴 리가 없습니다. 그쪽에서 뭔가 잘못된 것입니다.

B: 그럼, 차고로 연락해서 버스를 곧바로 공항으로 보내드리겠습니다. 1시간 정도 기다려 주시겠습니까?

T: 그렇게 오래 기다릴 수 없습니다. 모두들 매우 화가 나 있습니다. 버스를 취소하고 호텔까지 리무진버스로 가기로 하면 괜찮겠습니까?

B: 그렇게 하시겠다면 준비를 취소해 두겠습니다.

T: 힐튼 호텔로 오후 1시에 전화주십시오. 전 김이라고 합니다. 그때 잘못된 것이 있으면 의논하기로 하죠.

B: 예, 알겠습니다. 1시에 다시 전화 드리겠습니다. 감사합니다.

(2) 리무진버스의 이용

T: 힐튼 호텔행 리무진버스입니까?

L: 그렇습니다. 한 분입니까?

T: 아니오, 30명 단체입니다. 짐도 있습니다.

L: 짐을 이쪽을 가지고 오세요. 버스에 싣겠습니다.

T: 요금은 얼마입니까?

L: 호텔까지 1인당 5달러입니다. 지금 지불해주세요.

T: 30명분 150달러 여기 있습니다. 영수증을 받을 수 있겠습니까?

L: 호텔에 도착하는 대로 만들어서 드리겠습니다.
T: 좋습니다. 여기서 힐튼 호텔까지 얼마나 걸립니까?
L: 1시간 정도 걸립니다. (1시간 후에) 곧 힐튼 호텔에 도착할 것입니다. 그럼 즐거운 여행 되시길 바랍니다.
T: 예, 감사합니다.

(3) 렌터카 이용시

1) 렌터카 직원과의 대화(A)

R: 안녕하세요, 무엇을 도와드릴까요?
T: 안녕하세요, 차를 빌리고 싶습니다.
R: 얼마 동안 사용하시겠습니까?
T: 7일 동안 사용하겠습니다.
R: 어떤 모델을 원하십니까?
T: 브로슈어를 볼 수 있을까요?
R: 여기 있습니다.
T: (잠시 후) 이것으로 하겠습니다.
R: 좋습니다. 운전면허증과 신용카드 좀 보여주십시오.
T: 여기 있습니다. 국제자동차 운전면허증입니다.
R: 이 면허증말고 다른 신분증 가지고 계십니까?
T: 여권이 있습니다.
R: 좋습니다.
T: 요금은 얼마나 됩니까?
R: 전국적으로 정해져 있는 요금은 하루에 45달러이고, 마일당 20센트씩 추가됩니다.
T: 요금에 포함되어 있는 것은 무엇입니까?
R: 가스, 오일, 보험료 등이 포함되어 있고, 승차 회수와는 관계없습니다.
T: 차를 케네디 공항에서 반납할 수 있습니까?
R: 예, 그렇게 하실 수 있습니다. 보험은 어떻게 하시겠습니까?
T: 모두 포함 보험으로 부탁합니다. 지도 한 장 얻을 수 있습니까?
R: 물론입니다. 이 양식에 기입해주십시오. 지불은 어떻게 하시겠습니까?
T: 마스터 카드로 하겠습니다.
R: 운전에 주의하시고, 좌측통행에 주의를 해주십시오. 여기 차 열쇠와 영수증을 받으세요. 즐거운 여행이 되십시오.
T: 감사합니다.

2) 렌터카 직원과의 대화(B)

T: 오늘 차를 빌리고 싶은데요.
R: 예, 국제면허증 있으세요?
T: 예, 그러나 서울의 면허증을 사용하고 있습니다.

R: 좋습니다. 사륜구동 세단과 하드탑 중 어느 것을 하시겠어요?
T: 하드탑이 좋을 거 같은데요. 얼마인가요?
R: 여기에 요금표가 있습니다.
T: 보험료와 기름도 포함되어 있는 건가요?
R: 물론입니다.
T: 좋습니다. 하드탑으로 하겠습니다.
R: 신용카드로 하겠어요, 현금으로 하겠어요?
T: 현금으로 하겠어요.
R: 몇 시간 동안 이용하시겠어요.
T: 오전 9시부터 오후 6시까지 이용하고 싶습니다.

4. 버스에서의 안내

(1) 호텔로 향하는 도중 현지 여행사 직원의 안내

L: 안녕하세요, 여러분. 뉴욕에 오신 것을 환영하며, 만나뵙게 되어서 대단히 반갑습니다. 저는 글로벌 여행사에서 온 김영수입니다. 뉴욕에서 아주 좋은 시간을 가지시길 희망합니다. 저는 여러분들이 여기 계시는 동안 모든 서비스를 제공할 것입니다. 대단히 감사합니다.
T: 감사합니다. 미스터 김. 공항에서 힐튼 호텔까지는 얼마나 걸리나요?
L: 약 50분 정도 걸립니다.
T: 여기서 조금 멀군요.
L: 예. 이것은 새로운 여행일정표입니다. 다시 한번 살펴보십시오. 만약 변경사항이 있으시면 저에게 알려주십시오.
T: 너무 감사합니다. 그렇게 하겠습니다.

Chapter 3. 호텔에서의 영어

1. 예 약

(1) 호텔 객실 예약

1) 호텔 직원과의 대화(A)

O: 힐튼 호텔입니다. 무엇을 도와드릴까요?
T: 안녕하세요. 예약센터를 부탁합니다.
O: 잠시만 기다리십시오. 예약센터로 연결해 드리겠습니다.
R: 안녕하십니까, 힐튼 호텔 예약센터입니다. 무엇을 도와드릴까요?

T: 예, 저는 인솔자입니다. 저희 손님들을 위해서 객실을 예약하고 싶습니다.
R: 예, 손님. 언제 도착하십니까?
T: 우리는 9월 29일, 다음주 월요일에 도착합니다.
R: 29일 월요일이요. 며칠 동안 머물길 원하십니까?
T: 5일 동안 사용하길 원합니다.
R: 어떤 방을 원하십니까?
T: 더블룸 12개, 싱글룸 6개를 원합니다.
R: 예, 가능합니다.
T: 방마다 욕실은 있습니까?
R: 더블룸에는 목욕실이 있습니다만 싱글룸에는 샤워시설만 있습니다.
T: 좋습니다. 그리고 바다가 보이는 객실로 사용할 수 있습니까?
R: 오, 죄송합니다만 저희는 바다가 보이는 객실이 없습니다. 대신 매우 조용한 객실은 있습니다, 손님.
T: 좋습니다. 그것으로 하겠습니다. 객실 요금은 어떻게 됩니까?
R: 더블룸은 하룻밤에 85달러, 싱글룸은 하룻밤에 75달러입니다.
T: 서비스 요금과 세금을 포함한 가격입니까?
R: 물론입니다, 손님.
T: 좋습니다.
R: 성함과 전화번호를 말씀해주십시오.
T: 김입니다. 전화번호는 02-555-6482입니다.
R: 예, 알겠습니다, 미스터 김. 예약해주셔서 감사합니다. 변경사항이 있으시면 연락해주십시오. 곧 만나기를 기대합니다.

2) 호텔 직원과의 대화(B)

O: 워커힐입니다. 무엇을 도와드릴까요?
T: 예약부 부탁합니다.
O: 감사합니다. 예약부로 곧 연결해 드리겠습니다.
R: 예약부의 줄리입니다. 무엇을 도와드릴까요?
T: 예, 1월 21일부터 24일까지 3일밤 동안 싱글룸을 예약하고 싶습니다.
R: 잠시만 기다리세요. 예, 좋습니다. 성함과 전화번호를 알려주세요.
T: 이름은 김이고, 전화번호는 497-6829입니다.
R: 전화주셔서 감사합니다.

3) 호텔 직원과의 대화(C)

R: 무엇을 도와드릴까요?
T: 싱글룸을 예약하고 싶습니다.
R: 예, 언제로 예약을 해드릴까요?
T: 오늘밤이요. 빈 객실이 있을까요?
R: 예, 있습니다.
T: 적당한 객실로 주세요.

R: 4층 계단 옆에 하나 있습니다.
T: 시끄럽지 않을까요?
R: 조금 시끄럽지만 방음이 잘 되어서 괜찮습니다.
T: 좋습니다. 지금 같아서는 너무 피곤해서 길거리에서라도 잘 수 있을 거 같습니다. 그것으로 하겠습니다.
R: 예, 며칠 동안 머무실 건가요?
T: 이틀밤 동안 있을 겁니다. 하지만 오늘밤 있어보고 시끄러우면 내일 다른 객실로 옮길 수 있지요?
R: 물론입니다. 체크아웃시간은 오후 12입니다.

4) 호텔 직원과의 대화(D)

R: 예약부의 우마입니다. 무엇을 도와드릴까요?
T: 여기는 보스턴 공항인데요. 하루에 80달러하는 트윈룸을 월요일부터 목요일까지 예약하고 싶습니다. 그 가격에 맞는 방이 있을까요?
R: 예, 있습니다.
T: 잘 되었군요.
R: 성함을 말씀해주세요.
T: 김준호입니다.
R: 철자가 어떻게 되지요?
T: 성은 K-I-M이고, 이름은 J-U-N-H-O입니다.
R: 감사합니다, 손님. 언제 도착하실 건가요?
T: 지금 공항 리무진버스를 타고가는 중이니까 곧 도착할 겁니다. 그런데 호텔로 가는 가장 좋은 방법은 뭔지 좀 알려주시겠어요?
R: 예, 버스터미널에서 오른쪽으로 나와서 택시를 타시면 됩니다.

5) 호텔 직원과의 대화(E)

R: 예약부의 줄리입니다. 무엇을 도와드릴까요?
T: 예, 1월 29일에 어른 8명과 아이 9명분의 객실을 예약하고 싶습니다.
R: 며칠 동안 머물 예정인가요?
T: 4일 동안이요.
R: 예, 트윈룸과 그곳에 추가 베드를 넣어 드리겠습니다. 괜찮으시겠어요?
T: 좋습니다. 그리고 요금은 어떻게 되나요?
R: 아이들은 몇 살인가요?
T: 2명은 초등학생이고, 나머지는 7살 아래입니다.
R: 7살 아래는 하룻밤에 10달러씩 추가분을 내셔야 하고, 초등학생은 성인 요금의 반을 내셔야 합니다. 그리고 하룻밤 150달러에 아침식사는 포함됩니다.
T: 좋습니다.

(2) 호텔 객실의 예약이 안 되었을 경우

F: 안녕하세요, 무엇을 도와드릴까요?

T: 예, 체크인하기를 원합니다.
F: 성함이 어떻게 되십니까?
T: 해피 투어에서 온 김입니다.
F: 잠시만 기다리십시오. 이런, 죄송하지만 손님의 예약건에 대해 확인을 할 수가 없습니다. 언제 예약을 하셨습니까?
T: 오, 이런. 나의 여행사에서 1주일 전에 예약을 했습니다. 서울의 해피 투어입니다. 예약 명단에 없는 것이 확실합니까?
F: 다시 한번 확인해 보겠습니다. 죄송합니다만 예약이 되어 있지 않습니다.
T: 우리 일행은 뉴욕을 관광하기 위해서 왔습니다. 투숙 가능한 객실이 없을까요?
F: 없습니다. 오늘은 예약이 다 되어 있습니다.
T: 이럴 수가! 나의 여행사에서 확실히 예약을 했을 겁니다. 어떻게 해야 하나요?
F: 잠시만 기다리십시오. 매니저에게 전화를 해보겠습니다. 그가 손님과 손님의 일행을 위해서 좋은 방법을 제시할 것이라고 봅니다. 아마도 오늘 예약 취소된 객실이 있을 것입니다.
T: 그러기를 희망합니다.
F: 저쪽에 앉아서 기다려주십시오. 만약에 빈 객실이 없다면 매니저가 다른 호텔을 추천해줄 것입니다.

2. 체크인

(1) 호텔 체크인 중 객실 수가 잘못 예약되었을 때

F: 무엇을 도와드릴까요?
T: 예, 저는 해피 투어의 인솔자입니다. 우리는 방금 여기에 도착했는데 예약을 했습니다.
F: 기다리고 있었습니다. 손님. 해피 투어의 단원분들이시지요?
T: 예, 맞습니다.
F: 미스터 이입니까?
T: 아닙니다, 김입니다. 이는 나의 여행사의 사장입니다.
F: 오, 죄송합니다. 미스터 김. 힐튼 호텔에 오신 것을 환영합니다.
T: 감사합니다.
F: 일행은 모두 32명입니까?
T: 오, 아닙니다. 30명입니다.
F: 저희는 32명을 위한 11개의 더블룸과 10개의 싱글룸을 준비해 두었습니다.
T: 무언가 잘못되었습니다. 우리는 12개의 더블룸과 6개의 싱글룸을 해피 투어로 예약했습니다. 인환증에도 12개의 더블룸, 6개의 싱글룸으로 되어 있습니다. 모두 30명입니다.
F: 맞습니다. 손님. 30명을 위한 12개의 더블룸과 6개의 싱글룸을 드리겠습니다. 그리고 여기에 방 배정표도 있습니다.

T: 감사합니다.
F: 죄송합니다만 더블룸 중 두 개는 욕실이 없습니다.
T: 오, 이런! 욕실이 있는 다른 방은 없습니까?
F: 너무 죄송합니다만 샤워시설만 사용할 수 있는 객실밖에 남아 있지 않습니다.
T: 샤워시설은 있습니까?
F: 예. 샤워시설은 있습니다만 욕실은 없습니다. 오늘은 이 객실을 사용하시겠습니까? 내일부터는 다른 객실로 바꿔 드리겠습니다.
T: 내일 욕실이 있는 객실로 꼭 변경해주십시오.
F: 물론입니다. 손님. 불편을 드려서 죄송합니다.
T: 괜찮습니다.
F: 5일 동안 여기서 머물 예정입니까?
T: 맞습니다. 금요일에 체크아웃할 것입니다.
F: 좋습니다. 마스터 어카운트에 손님의 객실을 등록해도 되겠습니까?
T: 물론입니다. 되었지요?
F: 감사합니다, 손님. 여기에 열쇠가 있습니다.
T: 객실 하나당 열쇠 하나입니까?
F: 아닙니다. 한 명당 하나씩입니다.
T: 감사합니다.

(2) 호텔 체크인(A)

F: 안녕하십니까, 무엇을 도와드릴까요?
T: 예, 저는 해피 투어에서 온 인솔자입니다.
F: 반갑습니다, 손님. 성함이 어떻게 되십니까?
T: 김입니다. 김이 성입니다.
F: 예, 미스터 김. 예약 카드를 가지고 계십니까?
T: 여기에 있습니다.
F: 여기서는 글로벌 여행사로 예약을 하셨고, 12개의 더블룸, 6개의 싱글룸이 9월 29일부터 10월 3일까지 예약이 되어 있습니다. 모든 정확한가요, 미스터 김?
T: 예, 모두 정확합니다.
F: 이 숙박 카드에 좀 기입해 주시겠습니까?
T: 물론입니다. 여기 있습니다. 요금 지불은 언제 합니까? 지금입니까, 체크아웃 때입니까?
F: 체크아웃 때 하시면 됩니다. 지불은 어떻게 하시겠습니까?
T: 여행자 수표로 하겠습니다. 내일 아침 7시에 모닝콜 좀 걸어주시겠어요?
F: 좋습니다.
T: 감사합니다.
F: 늦게 퇴실하실 수 있는 시간은 3시까지이고, 25달러가 추가로 부과됩니다. 여기에 열쇠가 있습니다. 그리고 벨맨이 손님의 짐을 운반해줄 것입니다. 좋은 하루 되십시오.

(3) 호텔 체크인(B)

T: 포터를 불러주세요. 호텔 안으로 옮길 짐이 30개가 있어요.
D: 알겠습니다. 포터는 여기에 있습니다. 짐들은 가져오라고 말해놓겠습니다.
T: 고맙습니다. 프런트는 어디입니까?
D: 곧장 가셔서 계단으로 내려가면 그곳이 프런트입니다.
T: (프런트 클락에게) 단체 체크인은 어느 분이 담당하십니까?
F: 잠시만 기다려주십시오. 담당자가 있는지 보고 오겠습니다. 마침 있군요. 피터! 손님입니다.
F: 안녕하십니까? 저는 단체 담당의 피터 팬입니다. 무엇을 도와드릴까요?
T: 안녕하세요, 미스터 팬, 한국에서 온 해피 투어의 인솔자인 김입니다. 이곳의 객실 예약은 글로벌 여행사의 시카고 사무실에서 해놓았습니다.
F: 잠깐만 기다려주십시오. 예약 장부들을 살펴보겠습니다. 여기 있습니다. 손님의 단체는 30명이고, 트윈 13실과 싱글 4실에 각각 욕실이 딸린 방이죠?
T: 예, 그렇습니다. 숙박자 명단은 여기 있습니다.
F: 객실 배정에는 바뀐 사항이 있습니까?
T: 지금까지는 바뀐 사항이 없습니다. 객실은 똑같은 크기입니까? 열쇠를 단원에게 나누어주기 전에 확인하고 싶습니다.
F: 객실은 전부 똑같은 크기입니다.
T: 좋습니다. 그러면 열쇠를 주십시오.
T: 열쇠는 여기 있습니다. 싱글 4실의 열쇠 4개, 트윈 13실에 열쇠 26개 있습니다. 벨 캡틴에게 짐들을 객실로 옮기도록 하겠습니다.
B: 짐들은 전부 파란색 명찰이 있군요. 잘 운반하겠습니다.
T: 단원 중에 김씨가 두 명 있기 때문에 바뀌지 않게 해주십시오.
B: 알겠습니다. 바뀌지 않도록 하겠습니다.

(4) 예약 변경을 하지 않았을 때의 체크인

T: 3명이 줄어서 전원 27명이 되었습니다. 미리 알려드려야 했습니다만 도중에 시간이 없었습니다.
F: 알겠습니다. 객실은 몇 개가 필요하십니까?
T: 트윈 12실과 싱글 3실, 합계 15실입니다.
F: 마지막 명단은 어떻게 되었는지 가르쳐주십시오.
T: 명단에서 두번째 줄의 이름과 끝에서 두번째 줄과 세번째 줄의 이름을 명단에서 지워주십시오.
F: 객실 배정은 어떻게 됩니까?
T: 원래 싱글의 미스터 박께서 미스터 윤과 트윈룸을 사용하고 싶어하십니다. 결국 투어 참가를 그만둔 미스터 이 대신에 미스터 박이 들어가게 된 것입니다. 우리들은 트윈 1실과 싱글 1실을 사용하지 않아도 됩니다.
T: (시간이 조금 지나고 나서) 단원 중의 미스터 최로부터 객실이 시끄럽다는 불

만이 있었습니다. 객실번호는 1462호이고, 큰길 쪽으로 향하고 있기 때문에 자동차들의 소음이 굉장히 시끄럽다고 합니다. 객실을 바꿀 수 있을까요?

F: 14층 전부 만실입니다. 15층은 어떻습니까? 15층의 객실은 더 크고 조용한 객실이고 주택단지를 내려다볼 수 있는 곳입니다만 요금이 조금 비쌉니다.

T: 얼마를 더 내야 됩니까?

F: 하루에 5달러씩 추가됩니다.

T: 저희들이 객실료로 3일간 전부 800달러를 그쪽에 지불해야만 합니다. 1일 5달러 추가요금을 그쪽에서 빼주시지 않겠습니까?

F: 지배인과 상담하고 나서 바로 답변해 드리겠습니다.

T: 좋습니다. 그러면 미스터 최는 언제 객실을 바꿀 수 있습니까?

F: 10분 정도 기다려주십시오. 제가 알아보겠습니다.

T: 10분 후에 전화해주십시오.

F: 미스터 최는 객실을 15층 1516호로 옮기셔도 좋습니다. 추가요금은 없습니다.

3. 객실 배정

(1) 벨 캡틴과 변경된 방에 대해 이야기할 때 사용하는 회화

T: 안녕하세요, 전 인솔자입니다.

B: 안녕하세요, 손님.

T: 이것은 우리 일행의 짐입니다. 짐 몇 개를 받으셨나요?

B: 30개를 받았습니다.

T: 좋습니다. 목록을 가지고 있지요?

B: 예, 가지고 있습니다.

T: 한 가지 변경사항이 있습니다.

B: 어떤 것을 변경하시기 원하십니까?

T: 1417호실을 하나 더 배정받았습니다. 1524호실의 최씨 부부를 그곳에 기입해 주시겠습니까?

B: 알겠습니다. 다른 변경사항은 없으십니까?

T: 없습니다. 각각의 짐에 객실번호 기입하는 것을 도와드릴까요?

B: 감사합니다만 거의 끝났습니다.

T: 객실에 짐을 운반하는 데는 얼마나 걸립니까?

B: 1417호를 제외하고는 모든 객실이 같은 층에 있어서 30분 이상 걸리지는 않을 것입니다.

T: 가능하면 빨리 운반해 주시겠습니까?

B: 물론입니다. 최선을 다할 것입니다.

T: 감사합니다.

4. 벨맨 서비스

(1) 짐의 배달

F: 벨맨을 불러 가방 운반을 도와드리도록 하겠습니다. 미스터 김과 그의 일행들에게 객실을 안내해주세요.
B: 예, 이것이 모두 손님의 짐입니까?
T: 예, 그렇습니다.
B: 그리고 다른 짐은 오고 있습니까?
T: 예, 6개가 더 오고 있습니다.
B: 짐이 몇 개나 됩니까, 손님?
T: 30개입니다.
B: 알겠습니다. 객실 열쇠를 보여 주시겠습니까?
T: 여기 있습니다.
B: 손님의 객실은 15층에 있습니다. 제가 지금 안내해 드리겠습니다. 이쪽으로 오십시오. 발 밑을 조심하십시오. 왼쪽에 있는 엘리베이터를 타십시오.
T: 감사합니다. 호텔이 참 좋군요. 객실도 멋있습니다.
B: 감사합니다, 손님. 객실에 다 왔습니다. 짐은 어디다 놓아둘까요?
T: 저쪽 창가에다 두십시오.
B: 예, 호수의 전망이 참 좋습니다. 제가 객실 안내를 해드리겠습니다. 여기에 욕실 전등 스위치가 있고, 저기에 있는 나이트 테이블에는 객실 전등, 라디오, 에어컨디셔너의 스위치가 있습니다.
T: 예, 알겠습니다.
B: 옷장은 이쪽에 있고, 욕실은 저쪽에 있습니다. 냉장고와 술, 맥주, 음료수가 있는 미니바는 바로 이쪽에 있습니다. 모든 문구류는 책상 서랍에 있습니다.
T: 모두 무료입니까?
B: 아닙니다, 손님. 술과 음료는 모두 퇴실하실 때 요금을 지불하셔야 합니다.
T: 알겠습니다. 그리고 룸서비스 담당자는 어떻게 부릅니까?
B: 전화를 사용하셔서 9번을 누르시면 프런트 데스크, 2번을 누르시면 룸서비스, 3번을 누르시면 벨 캡틴이 연결됩니다. 룸서비스 메뉴와 호텔의 편의시설을 볼 수 있는 브로슈어는 책상 위에 있습니다. 저희 룸서비스는 24시간 운영하고 있으므로 언제든지 사용하실 수 있습니다.
T: 오, 알겠습니다. 바는 언제까지 운영합니까?
B: 1층에 있는 바 테라스는 저녁 11시 40분까지 운영합니다. 테이블을 예약해드릴까요?
T: 예, 그렇게 해주십시오. 저녁 8시에 우리는 그곳에서 휴식시간을 갖길 원합니다.
B: 알겠습니다, 손님.
T: 감사합니다. 여기 팁이 있습니다.
B: 죄송합니다만 팁은 받을 수가 없게 되어 있습니다. 손님의 영수증에 봉사요금이 포함되어 나올 것입니다.

T: 여하튼 고맙습니다.
B: 천만에 말씀이십니다. 필요한 것이 있으시면 언제든지 불러주십시오.

(2) 잘못된 짐의 배달

B: (문을 노크하며) 안녕하세요, 여기 손님의 짐이 있습니다.
T: 예, 들어오세요.
B: 여기에 30개의 짐이 있습니다. 모두 맞는지 확인해보십시오.
T: 예, 30개가 전부지요. 한번 봅시다. 이런, 이 짐 중에 2개는 우리의 짐이 아닙니다.
B: 확실합니까, 손님? 제가 다른 짐 두 개를 가져왔군요.
T: 예, 확실히 저희 짐이 아닙니다. 모든 짐에는 노란색 짐표가 붙어 있습니다. 하지만 이것은 다른 짐표가 붙어 있습니다. 아마도 당신이 실수한 거 같습니다.
B: 죄송합니다. 제가 실수를 한 것 같습니다. 벨 캡틴에게 다시 한번 확인해보고 손님의 짐을 가지고 곧 돌아오겠습니다.
T: 예, 서둘러주십시오. 그리고 객실문은 저절로 잠깁니까?
B: 예 저절로 잠깁니다. 그러므로 객실을 나서실 때는 열쇠를 꼭 가지고가시는 것을 잊지 마십시오.

5. 체크아웃할 때의 짐 서비스

B: 안녕하십니까, 벨 캡틴입니다. 무엇을 도와드릴까요?
T: 예, 저는 인솔자입니다. 우리는 떠날 준비가 다 되었습니다. 1512호로 한 명 보내주시겠습니까? 우리 일행의 모든 짐은 저의 객실에 있습니다.
B: 알겠습니다. 곧 보내 드리겠습니다.
(벨맨이 곧 1512호로 와서 모든 짐들을 로비로 운반하였다)
B: 이것이 모두 전부입니까?
T: 예, 30개가 전부입니다. 한번 확인해보십시오.
B: 정확합니다. 택시를 잡아드릴까요?
T: 아니오, 괜찮습니다. 우리는 버스를 탈 것입니다. 버스까지 짐을 운반해 주시겠습니까?
B: 예, 알겠습니다. 좋은 여행 되시고, 또다시 방문해주십시오.
T: 감사합니다.

6. 객실 내에서의 여러 서비스

(1) 장거리 전화 서비스

O: 교환입니다. 무엇을 도와드릴까요?

T: 1512호의 미스터 김입니다. 시카고로 장거리 전화를 걸고 싶습니다. 야간 요금이 붙습니까?
O: 예, 저녁 8시부터 아침 6시까지 야간 요금이 붙습니다.
T: 시카고는 지금 몇 시입니까?
O: 1시간 정도 차이가 나므로 지금 8시 20분입니다.
T: 좋습니다. 지금 전화를 걸고 싶습니다.
O: 예, 잠시만 기다려주십시오. 장거리 교환으로 연결해 드리겠습니다.
T: 전화요금은 영수증에 함께 포함되는 걸 원치 않습니다. 그래서 제 카드로 요금을 지불하고 싶습니다.
O: 예, 카드번호가 어떻게 됩니까?
T: 마스터 카드이고, 번호는 27138298입니다.
O: 감사합니다, 손님. 장거리 교환에 연결해드리고, 나중에 요금에 대해서 알려드리겠습니다.
T: 지금 곧 전화 연결이 가능합니까?
O: 그럴 것입니다만 만약에 회선이 모두 사용중이면 조금 기다리셔야 합니다.
T: 오랫동안 기다릴 수가 없습니다. 우리는 나가야 하므로 서둘러야 합니다.
O: 예, 잠시만 기다리십시오. 지금 장거리 교환과 연결되었습니다. 끊지 말고 기다리십시오. 장거리 교환, 힐튼 호텔 1512호의 미스터 김이 장거리 전화를 원하고, 신용카드로 요금을 지불하길 원합니다.
L: 누구와 전화하길 원합니까, 미스터 김?
T: 시카고에 있는 미스터 최와 통화하고 싶습니다. 지역번호는 773, 전화번호는 619-6489입니다. 요금은 제 신용카드로 지불하겠습니다.
L: 전화를 끊어주십시오. 제가 잠시 후에 다시 전화를 드리겠습니다. (몇 분 후) 전화가 연결되었습니다. 미스터 김, 말씀하십시오.

(2) 모닝콜을 부탁할 때

O: 교환입니다. 무엇을 도와드릴까요?
T: 해피 투어의 미스터 김입니다. 내일 아침 6시 30분에 우리 일행들에게 모닝콜 좀 해주시겠습니까?
O: 예, 미스터 김. 아침 6시 30분에 모닝콜을 해드리겠습니다. 좋은 밤 되십시오.
T: 감사합니다.

(3) 하우스키핑

1) 객실을 청소하기 위하여 하우스키퍼가 방문할 때

M: (문을 노크하며) 계십니까?
T: 예, 무슨 일입니까?
M: 제가 방을 청소하러 들어가도 되겠습니까?
T: 지금은 말고, 이따 다시 오겠습니까? 전 11시에 나갈 것입니다.

M: 예, 손님. 방해해서 죄송합니다.
T: 괜찮아요. "방해하지 마시오"라는 표시를 걸어 두어야겠군요.
M: 예, 그러면 아무도 방해하지 않을 겁니다. 만약 청소를 원하시면 "청소 부탁합니다"라는 표시를 걸어주십시오.
T: 알겠습니다. 그렇게 하겠습니다. 어쨌든 감사합니다.

2) 메이드 서비스를 부탁할 때

H: 하우스키핑입니다. 무엇을 도와드릴까요?
T: 예, 저의 방으로 누구 좀 보내주십시오.
H: 예, 몇 호실입니까, 손님?
T: 1512호입니다. 욕실을 청소했으면 합니다.
H: 예, 메이드를 곧 보내 드리겠습니다. 그밖에 다른 사항들은 없으십니까?
T: 목욕 수건 2장이 필요합니다. 그리고 1417호의 미스터 이의 데스크 램프를 수리할 사람도 보내주십시오. 램프가 좀 어둡습니다.
H: 곧 손님과 미스터 이의 객실로 사람을 보내겠습니다.
T: 감사합니다. 또한 미스터 이의 아이를 위해서 여분의 침대 커버와 담요도 주시겠습니까?
H: 물론 보내 드리겠습니다.
T: 좋습니다. 감사합니다.

(4) 세탁 서비스

1) 세탁물을 서비스받을 때(A)

L: 안녕하십니까, 하우스키핑입니다. 무엇을 도와드릴까요?
T: 1514호에 있는 인솔자 미스터 송입니다. 우리 일행 중 몇 명이 세탁 서비스를 받기 원합니다. 모든 세탁물은 저의 방에 있습니다. 이곳으로 직원을 보내주시겠습니까?
L: 예, 곧 직원을 보내겠습니다.
T: 그 동안 무엇을 해야 합니까?
L: 세탁물 넣는 봉투에 세탁물을 넣으시고, 세탁물과 드라이클리닝 전표에 세탁 목록을 기입해주십시오.
T: 세탁물 봉투는 어디에 있습니까?
L: 옷장 안에 전표와 함께 있습니다.
T: 아, 알겠습니다. 만약 오늘 세탁물을 맡기면 언제 찾을 수 있습니까?
L: 급하십니까?
T: 아니오, 그렇지는 않지만 우리는 모레 오전에 이곳을 떠납니다.
L: 일반적으로 내일 낮에는 세탁물을 받으실 수 있으시지만 아주 급하다면 급행으로 세탁하여 오늘 저녁에 받으실 수 있으십니다. 그렇게 하시면 비용을 조금 더 내셔야 합니다.
T: 그렇게 급하지는 않습니다.

L: 좋습니다. 곧 직원을 보내 드리겠습니다. (잠시 후) 세탁 서비스입니다. 안녕하십니까? 손님.
T: 들어오세요. 이곳에 기입할 때까지 그리 오래 걸리지는 않으니 잠시만 기다리십시오.
L: 예, 손님.
T: 여기에 있습니다. 자켓 2장, 블라우스 3장, 그리고 바지 5장입니다. 정확한지 한번 체크해보십시오.
L: (다시 확인한 후) 손님은 여기에 블라우스 3장이라고 쓰셨는데 세탁물에는 2장밖에 없습니다.
T: 진짜요? 제가 다시 한번 확인해 보겠습니다. 아, 나머지 한 장이 카펫 위에 떨어졌군요. 자, 여기에 있습니다. 이제 정확하지요?
L: 예, 맞습니다. 세탁물이 급하게 필요하지는 않다고 하셨지요?
T: 아닙니다. 내일 오후까지는 끝내주십시오. 가능하시지요?
L: 예, 오후 5시까지 보내 드리겠습니다.
T: 좋습니다. 그리고 이 블라우스에 있는 얼룩을 꼭 지워주십시오.
L: 이것이 무슨 얼룩입니까?
T: 칠리 소스 얼룩인 것 같습니다.
L: 음, 제가 할 수 있는 데까지 해보겠습니다.
T: 잘 되기를 바라겠습니다.

2) 세탁물을 서비스받을 때(B)

T: 안녕하세요, 여기는 1872호인데요. 셔츠 두 개와 속옷 몇 개는 세탁하고, 양복 한 벌은 클리닝한 후 다림질 부탁합니다. 지금 올라오실 수 있지요?
L: 예, 곧 가겠습니다.
T: 언제 찾을 수 있나요?
L: 양복은 내일 오전까지면 되고, 통상 서비스를 이용하면 세탁물은 내일 오후 5시까지면 됩니다. 괜찮으시겠어요?
T: 괜찮습니다.
L: 곧 올라가겠습니다.

3) 세탁한 세탁물을 받을 때(C)

L: 안녕하십니까? 세탁 서비스입니다, 손님.
T: 들어오세요.
L: 손님의 세탁물을 가지고 왔습니다.
T: 세탁은 잘되었나요? 칠리 소스 얼룩은 지워졌나요?
L: 예, 만족할 만큼 잘 세탁되었다고 믿습니다. 한번 확인해 보시겠습니까? 여기에 세탁물과 어제 사인하신 전표가 있습니다. 자세히 보십시오.
T: 정확한 거 같군요. (세탁물 확인 후) 모두 정확합니다. 감사합니다.
L: 천만에 말씀이십니다. 여기에 청구서가 있습니다. 어떻게 지불하시겠습니까?
T: 호텔 인환증으로 하겠습니다. 어디에 서명을 하지요?
L: 여기 있습니다. 이곳에 서명하시면 됩니다. 감사합니다.

7. 안내 데스크에서 안내를 받을 때

I: 안녕하십니까, 무엇을 도와드릴까요?
T: 예, 제 디지털 카메라를 수리하고 싶은데요. 수리점이 이 근처에 있습니까?
I: 카메라 수리는 호텔의 선물상점에서 하실 수 있습니다. 꽃상점이 있는 복도를 쭉 따라가시면 그랜드 바 옆에 위치해 있습니다.
T: 매우 편리하네요. 그리고 우리 일행들은 도시관광을 하고 싶어합니다. 그들을 위해서 도시관광 버스를 준비해 주시겠습니까?
I: 물론입니다, 손님. 제가 손님을 위해서 대신 처리해 두겠습니다. 일행이 몇 분이십니까?
T: 30명입니다.
I: 여기에 버스 투어에 관한 브로슈어가 있습니다.
T: 감사합니다. 가격은 얼마입니까?
I: 손님이 선택하시는 것에 따라 가격이 달라집니다. 오전 9시부터 12시까지 하는 오전 투어는 30달러이고, 오후 1시부터 4시까지 더 많은 장소를 관광하는 오후 투어는 35달러입니다. 그리고 저녁 7시부터 11시까지 하는 나이트 투어는 50달러입니다.
T: 오후 투어와 나이트 투어의 차이점은 무엇입니까?
I: 나이트 투어는 가장 인기 있는 투어입니다. 그것에는 극장, 바, 그리고 할인된 가격으로 이용할 수 있는 다른 장소들이 포함되어 있습니다.
T: 많은 정보 감사드립니다. 브로슈어를 좀더 본 후에 결정을 하겠습니다.

8. 호텔 내에서의 식사

(1) 아침식사

W: 안녕하십니까? 주문하시겠습니까, 손님?
T: 예, 미국식 아침식사를 원합니다.
W: 예, 손님. 주스는 어떤 것으로 선택하시겠습니까? 저희는 오렌지, 토마토, 망고 주스를 준비해두고 있습니다.
T: 망고 주스로 하겠습니다.
W: 예, 계란 두 개를 원하시는 조리법대로 선택하실 수 있습니다. 삶아드릴까요, 프라이를 해드릴까요?
T: 프라이 해주십시오.
W: 한 쪽만 프라이를 해드릴까요, 양쪽 다 해드릴까요?
T: 한 쪽만 해주십시오.
W: 알겠습니다. 그리고 소시지와 베이컨 중에 선택하실 수 있습니다.
T: 베이컨으로 하겠습니다. 바삭바삭하게 해주십시오.
W: 예, 손님. 그리고 메시드 포테이토와 시리얼 중 어느 것을 선택하시겠습니까?

T: 어떤 종류의 시리얼이 있습니까?
W: 콘 프레이크, 쉐드 윗, 퍼프드 라이스, 그리고 오트밀이 있습니다.
T: 오트밀로 하겠습니다. 그리고 토스트는 살짝만 구워주십시오.
W: 예, 알겠습니다. 커피와 차 중 어느 것으로 하시겠습니까?
T: 밀크 티로 하겠습니다. 그리고 서둘러 주십시오. 9시까지는 공항에 가야 합니다.
W: 알겠습니다, 손님. 곧 가져오겠습니다.

(2) 룸서비스로 주문시

1) 룸서비스로 아침식사 주문시(A)

R: 룸서비스입니다. 무엇을 도와드릴까요?
T: 예, 아침식사 주문하기에 시간이 늦었습니까?
R: 아닙니다. 룸서비스는 24시간 계속 운영하고 있습니다.
T: 좋습니다. 영국식 아침식사 가능합니까?
R: 물론입니다. 손님. 시리얼과 과일 주스 중 어느 것을 원하십니까?
T: 오렌지 주스로 주십시오.
R: 커피와 홍차가 있습니다. 어느 것을 원하십니까?
T: 우유를 탄 커피로 주십시오. 그리고 프렌치 프라이가 아닌 양파를 곁들인 치즈버거 2개, 베이컨, 양상치, 토마토를 넣은 샌드위치 3개, 햄과 계란 샌드위치 1개를 주십시오.
R: 양파를 곁들인 치즈버거 2개, 베이컨, 양상치, 토마토를 넣은 샌드위치 3개, 햄과 계란 샌드위치 1개가 전부입니까, 손님?
T: 마실 것도 필요합니다. 아이스티 5잔, 플레인 소다 3병을 주십시오.
R: 알겠습니다. 몇 호실입니까?
T: 1415호입니다.
R: 1415호. 15분 정도 걸릴 것입니다.
T: 좋습니다. 감사합니다.

2) 룸서비스로 아침식사 주문시(B)

R: 룸서비스입니다.
T: 햄 샌드위치하고 커피를 주문하고 싶습니다. 여기는 1209호입니다.
R: 감사합니다. 15분 정도 걸리니 기다려 주시겠습니까? (노크하며) 미스터 김의 방입니까? 룸서비스입니다.
T: 네, 들어오세요. 문 열려 있습니다.
R: 안녕하세요, 손님. 아침이 준비 다 되었습니다. 어디에다 놓을까요?
T: 테이블 위에 놓으십시오.
R: 알겠습니다. 여기 있습니다.
T: 그리고 차를 계속 따뜻하게 유지하고 싶습니다.
R: 차는 전기 여과기 안에 있습니다. 이 코드를 벽에 있는 소켓에 꽂으시면 계속 따뜻하게 유지할 수 있습니다.

T: 좋습니다.
R: 이 전표에 사인을 해주시겠습니까, 손님?
T: 물론입니다. 여기 있습니다. 다 먹고 나서 접시는 어떻게 할까요?
R: 바깥에 놓아두십시오.
T: 고맙습니다. 여기 팁입니다.

9. 호텔 안에서 물건을 분실했을 때

C: 안녕하세요, 무엇을 도와드릴까요?
T: 예, 우리 일행 중의 미시즈 신께서 그녀의 결혼반지를 잃어버렸습니다. 혹시 분실물 센터에 있습니까?
C: 제가 한번 확인해보겠습니다. 어떤 종류의 반지이며, 어떻게 생겼습니까?
T: 그녀의 말에 의하면 백금과 블루 사파이어로 되어 있는 반지이며, 하트 모양이라고 합니다. 그리고 반지 안에 그녀와 그녀의 남편 이름이 새겨져 있다고 합니다. 그 반지는 그녀가 남편에게서 받은 유일한 결혼반지라고 합니다. 그래서 그녀는 꼭 다시 찾기를 원합니다.
C: 오, 매우 중요한 반지군요. 잠시만 기다리십시오. 죄송합니다만 이곳에는 반지가 없는 것 같습니다. 그녀가 객실 안에 반지를 두지 않은 것은 확실합니까?
T: 예, 그녀의 방을 모두 찾아보았지만 그곳에는 없었습니다. 그리고 그녀가 쇼핑하러 방을 나설 때에도 반지를 손가락에 끼고 있었다고 합니다.
C: 그녀는 어디에서 쇼핑을 하셨습니까?
T: 호텔의 쇼핑 아케이드에서 했습니다. 그리고 쇼핑 후에는 호텔의 피트니스 센터에 갔다고 합니다.
C: 걱정하지 마십시오. 여기 분실 신고서에 기입해주시고, 만약 반지가 발견되면 손님에게 연락을 드리겠습니다.
T: 꼭 찾도록 해주십시오.
C: 예, 최선을 다하겠습니다. (1시간 후) 여보세요, 미스터 김. 분실물 센터 직원입니다. 좋은 소식입니다. 미시즈 신의 반지를 찾았습니다. 그녀는 피트니스 센터 탈의실에 반지를 떨어뜨렸습니다. 그곳 직원들이 안전하게 반지를 보관하고 있습니다.
T: 오, 도와주셔서 너무 감사합니다. 제가 곧 반지를 가지러 가겠습니다. 그리고 미시즈 신께서 당신께 감사의 말을 전하고 싶다고 그곳으로 가기를 원합니다.
C: 오, 그러실 필요 없습니다만 저의 데스크에서 뵙는다면 너무 기쁠 것입니다.
T: 다시 한번 감사합니다. 곧 뵙겠습니다.

10. 체크아웃

(1) 체크아웃(A)

F: 안녕하십니까, 무엇을 도와드릴까요?
T: 예, 체크아웃 시간이 언제입니까?
F: 정오까지입니다. 오늘 체크아웃하시겠습니까?
T: 예, 저는 해피 투어의 인솔자입니다. 우리는 저녁 비행기로 떠납니다. 5시까지 객실 두 개만 사용할 수 있습니까?
F: 죄송합니다. 만약 12시에 체크아웃을 안 하시면 하루치 숙박비를 더 내셔야 합니다.
T: 이럴 수가, 그렇게 할 수가 없습니다. 우리는 오직 5시간만 객실이 필요합니다. 특별한 배려를 해줄 수 없습니까?
F: 죄송합니다, 손님. 그것이 저희 호텔의 정책입니다. 그것을 깰 수는 없습니다. 만약 원하신다면 매니저에게 말씀드리는 것이 더 나을 것 같습니다.
T: 음, 만약 우리가 가능한 한 빨리 체크아웃하면 우리의 짐을 오후까지 맡아줄 수 있습니까?
F: 물론입니다. 저기의 벨 캡틴에게 맡기시면 잘 보관해드릴 것입니다.
T: 좋습니다. 그렇게 하겠습니다.
F: 큰 도움을 못 드려서 죄송합니다.
T: 괜찮습니다. 어쨌든 감사합니다.

(2) 체크아웃(B)

F: 안녕하세요, 무엇을 도와드릴까요?
T: 예, 872호실 체크아웃을 하고싶어요.
F: 알겠습니다, 손님. 계산서를 뽑아 드리겠습니다. 저희 호텔에서 즐거운 시간을 보내셨나요?
T: 예, 너무 즐거웠습니다. 다시 오겠습니다.
F: 감사합니다. 여기에 계산서가 있습니다.
T: 좋습니다. 신용카드도 되나요?
F: 물론입니다.
T: 어떤 종류의 신용카드를 받나요?
F: 모든 종류의 신용카드를 다 취급합니다.
T: 여기 마스터 카드요.
F: 여기에 사인을 해주세요. 공항까지 택시를 불러드릴까요?
T: 아니오, 괜찮아요. 공항버스를 타고갈 겁니다.
F: 좋습니다. 저희 호텔을 이용해주셔서 너무 감사합니다.

(3) 체크아웃시 정산

T: 저는 해피 투어의 인솔자입니다. 체크아웃을 하고 싶습니다.
F: 알겠습니다, 손님. 영수증을 드리겠습니다. 여기 있습니다.
T: 감사합니다. 한번 봅시다. 오 이런, 예상보다는 금액이 너무 많이 청구되었습니다.
F: 제가 각 항목에 대해서 설명해드릴까요?
T: 예, 'L'이라고 표시된 8달러는 무엇입니까?
F: 'L'은 장거리 전화 사용료입니다. 지난밤에 장거리 전화 사용을 하셨지요?
T: 예, 기억합니다. 이런, 너무 오랫동안 통화를 한 것 같군요. 그리고 여기의 'R'과 또 다른 'B'는 무엇입니까?
F: 'R'은 룸서비스입니다. 아마도 세탁 서비스를 사용하셨거나, 아니면 다른 룸서비스를 사용하신 것 같습니다.
T: 예, 맞습니다. 세탁 서비스를 받았습니다. 그리고 룸으로 주스와 버거 서비스를 받았습니다.
F: 'B'는 아침식사를 의미합니다.
T: 아, 예. 제가 알기로는 아침식사는 객실요금에 포함된 걸로 알고 있습니다.
F: 예, 맞습니다. 하지만 손님은 특별식을 이용하셨습니다.
F: 그리고 여기에 'L'은 점심식사를, 'D'는 저녁식사를 의미합니다.
T: 예, 영수증이 정확히 나온 것 같습니다. 정확한 설명 감사합니다.
F: 천만에 말씀이십니다. 지불은 어떻게 하시겠습니까? 카드로 하시겠습니까, 현금으로 하시겠습니까?
T: 카드로 하겠습니다.

(4) 체크아웃시 짐의 운반사항 문의

T: 내일 정오 우리 체크아웃하는 짐들을 부탁드리겠습니다.
B: 예, 그런데 내일 정오에는 제가 근무하지 않습니다. 사이먼이 당신들 짐을 담당할 것입니다.
T: 그럼 사이먼씨에게 내일 낮 9시에 우리 짐 30개가 나갈 것이라고 말해 주시겠습니까?
B: 물론입니다. 확실히 전달해 놓겠습니다. 용건을 메모로 해놓겠습니다.
T: 오전 9시에 짐을 모아주세요. 짐은 객실의 문밖에 놓겠습니다. 17실 전부 15층이고, 숙박명단에 있는 것처럼 1560호부터 1574호까지이고, 1583, 1585호입니다.
B: 잘 알겠습니다. 그밖에 다른 일은 없습니까?
T: 손으로 들 수 있는 짐들은 침대 위에 올려놓겠습니다. 침대 위의 있는 것들은 가져가지 마십시오. 단원들이 들고 나갈 것입니다.
B: (프런트 접수계에게 향해서) 내일 정오에 체크아웃할 것입니다. 단원들의 단체계산서와 그밖에 개인적으로 사용한 계산서도 9시까지 준비해주십시오.

F: 점심식사는 여기서 할 것입니까?
T: 점심식사 계산서는 커피숍에서 직접 계산하기 때문에 총계산서에는 포함시키지 마십시오.
F: 알겠습니다. 9시까지 전부 준비해 놓겠습니다.
T: 계산 정산은 9시에 하겠습니다. 그리고 2시간 정도 객실 1실을 저희가 사용할 수 있겠습니까? 공항에 가는 버스는 12시에 여기서 출발합니다. 2시간 동안이나 로비에서 기다릴 수가 없어서요.
F: 그것은 가능할 것 같습니다. 정오가 되면 환대 객실을 사용할 수 있을지 조사해보겠습니다.
T: 너무 친절하게 해주셔서 정말 감사합니다.
F: (체크아웃할 때 캐셔 데스크) 계산서는 모두 준비되어 있습니다. 확인해주십시오.
T: 좋습니다. 잠시만 기다려주십시오. 이 부분은 잘 모르겠는데요. 도착한 날 5인분의 저녁식사입니다. 도착한 날은 저녁 늦게 도착했기 때문에 식사를 할 수 없었을 겁니다. 계산서에는 본 적이 없는 한국어로 된 사인과 객실번호가 적혀 있습니다. 이것은 우리 계산서가 아닙니다.
F: 조사해 보겠습니다. 아, 그렇군요. 이 계산서는 깜박하고 손님의 계산서에 계산되어진 것 같습니다. 대단히 죄송합니다. 총계산서에서 그만큼을 제하고, 금방 새로운 계산서를 만들어 드리겠습니다.
T: 이번에는 정확하군요. 객실 열쇠를 돌려 드리겠습니다. 전부 30개입니다.

Chapter 4. 관광과 쇼핑

1.관광 전의 여러 의논사항

(1) 에이전트 사원과 의논

1) 당일 여행을 갈 경우 현지 에이전트 사원과의 미팅

T: 안녕하십니까, 저는 한국에서 온 해피 투어의 인솔자인 김입니다.
R: 만나서 반갑습니다, 미스터 김. 저는 뉴욕의 글로벌 여행사의 이입니다.
T: 예, 저도 만나서 반갑습니다. 저기 앉아서 여행일정을 확인합시다.
R: 예. (여정을 보여주며) 여행은 워싱턴 1일 여행입니다.
T: 언제, 어디서 출발합니까?
R: 아침 8시에 호텔에서 태워드립니다.
T: 그러면 언제 돌아오나요?
R: 저녁 6시쯤 돌아올 겁니다.
T: 예, 여기서 멉니까?
R: 아니오, 버스로 약 40분 정도 걸립니다.

T: 좋습니다.

2) **엑스카션의 구체적인 미팅 바우처 내용을 체크하면서 이야기를 진행**

T: 여기서부터 얼마나 멉니까?

R: 좀 먼 거리입니다. 아마도 4시간 정도 걸릴 겁니다.

T: 워싱턴까지 가는 도중에 내립니까?

R: 예, 여기서 40마일 정도 가서 필라델피아에서 휴식합니다. 그리고 40마일 더 가서 워싱턴에 도착합니다. 워싱턴에서는 룰레이 동굴을 견학합니다. 동굴을 싫어하시는 분들이라도 분명히 즐거운 여행이 될 것입니다.

T: 동굴은 얼마 정도 관광합니까?

R: 약 1시간 정도입니다.

T: 재미있을 것 같군요. 점심은 어떻게 됩니까? 룰레이 동굴 근처에서 먹습니까?

R: 예, 동굴 관광 후에 바로 먹습니다. 우리는 마켓 인에 예약을 해두었습니다. 그곳은 깨끗하고 저렴한 가격의 해물요리 전문점입니다. 여기서 버스로 20분 정도 걸립니다.

T: 인환증에는 중식이 포함되지 않아 있으므로 마켓 인에서는 저희가 직접 지불하는 것이지요?

R: 예, 맞습니다.

T: 레스토랑 좌석은 예약을 해야 합니까?

R: 제가 1시로 예약을 해놓았습니다. 그 시간에는 레스토랑은 붐비지 않습니다. 피크 시간대에는 피하고 있습니다.

T: 좋습니다. 워싱턴에서는 무엇을 관광합니까?

R: 여정대로 백안관, 스미스 소니언 박물관, 워싱턴 기념탑, 그리고 제퍼슨 기념관을 관람합니다.

T: 시내관광에 포함된 요금은 무엇입니까? 입장료는 관광요금에 포함되어 있습니까?

R: 아니오, 들어 있지 않습니다. 직접 그 장소에서 지불하십시오.

T: 박물관 입장료는 얼마입니까?

R: 어른은 1달러 50센트입니다.

T: 잘 알겠습니다. 그럼 내일 아침 7시 30분에 호텔 앞으로 버스를 준비해주십시오.

R: 예, 그렇게 하겠습니다. 내일 뵙겠습니다.

(2) 가이드, 운전사와의 의논

1) **가이드 서비스 내용을 확인**

G: 좋은 아침입니다. 뉴욕에 오신 걸 환영합니다. 저는 글로벌 여행사에서 온 이며, 운전사 겸 가이드입니다. 잘 부탁합니다.

T: 만나서 반갑습니다, 미스터 이. 전 해피 투어의 인솔자인 김입니다.

G: 오늘 워싱턴에서 즐거운 시간이 되길 바랍니다. 여러분들을 위해서 모든 서비스를 제공하겠습니다.

T: 감사합니다. 우리가 탈 버스는 어디에 있습니까?
R: 호텔 차고에 있습니다.
T: 알겠습니다. 7시 30분에 출발합시다.
G: 좋습니다. 여러분들은 영어를 하십니까?
T: 아니오, 잘 못하지만 당신이 천천히 이야기하면 알 것입니다. 당신이 하는 말은 제가 한국어로 여러분들에게 말하겠습니다.
G: 알겠습니다. 워싱턴 관광은 점심식사 후입니다. 오전 중에는 워싱턴으로 가는 도중에 이 나라의 남북전쟁에 대한 이야기를 하겠습니다. 여기서부터 약 4시간 가량 소요됩니다.
T: 재미있는 강연 여행이 되겠네요. 역사적인 사건에 대해서 이야기 할 때에는 너무 많이 이야기하지 마세요. 그리고 이야기 중간에 조금 틈을 주세요. 한국어로 통역할 테니까요. 괜찮겠습니까?
G: 예. 그렇게 하겠습니다.
T: 모두 모였습니다. 출발해도 되겠습니다.

2. 관 광

(1) 사전 관광예약

T: 여기서 관광예약을 하나요?
E: 예, 몇 명이신가요?
T: 25명이고, 도시 관광을 하고 싶어요.
E: 좋습니다.
T: 어떻게 관광을 하지요?
E: 버스로 합니다.
T: 혹시 한국어로 된 안내책자가 있나요?
E: 물론입니다. 안내책자를 원하세요?
T: 예, 그리고 여기서 볼 만한 장소를 좀 추천해주세요.

(2) 목적지에 도착해서 관광을 어떻게 진행시킬 것인가를 가이드와 미팅

G: 워싱턴에 도착했습니다. 우선 안내센터로 가서 워싱턴의 약도를 보겠습니다.
T: 센터에서는 그밖에 무엇을 볼 수 있습니까?
G: 안내서를 살 수도 있고 한국어 해설 소개영화를 볼 수 있습니다.
T: 한국어로 말입니까?
G: 예, 해설은 한국어 이외에도 6개 국어로 녹음되어 있습니다.
T: 워싱턴 안내책자 있습니까?
G: 있습니다. 버스에서 내려서 센터로 갑시다. 버스는 열쇠로 잠그는데 귀중품은 두지 마세요.

T: 예, 두지 않겠습니다.

3. 쇼 핑

(1) 쇼핑의 기본적인 회화

S: 무엇을 도와드릴까요?
K: 실례하지만 카메라는 어디서 살 수 있을까요?
S: 전자부는 7층에 있습니다. 에스컬레이터에서 내리면 왼쪽에 있습니다.
K: 에스컬레이터는 어디에 있나요?
S: 통로를 똑바로 내려가십시오. 오른쪽에 있습니다.
K: 감사합니다.
(전자부에서)
S: 무엇을 찾고 계십니까?
K: 저 카메라 좀 볼 수 있습니까?
S: 예, 이것 말씀이신가요?
K: 예, 그리고 다른 것도 보여주십시오.
S: 여기에 있습니다.
K: 감사합니다. 이것과 저것의 차이점은 무엇입니까?
S: 이것은 자동이고, 저것은 수동입니다.
K: 가격은 어떻게 되지요?
S: 이것은 300달러이고, 저것은 200달러입니다.
K: 이것으로 하겠습니다.
S: 현금입니까, 카드입니까?
K: 카드입니다.
S: 신분증을 볼 수 있을까요?
K: 여기에 여권이 있습니다.
S: 좋습니다. 여기에 손님 이름을 서명해주세요.
K: 예, 그리고 포장을 해주시겠습니까?
S: 저쪽 카운터로 가져가주세요.
K: 고맙습니다.

(2) 조금 복잡한 쇼핑의 경우

S: 무엇을 도와드릴까요?
T: 예, 셔츠를 찾고 있습니다.
S: 손님의 치수는 얼마입니까?
T: 중간 크기입니다.
S: 이것은 어떻습니까?

T: 제가 원하는 것이 아닙니다. 같은 물건으로 다른 색상은 없습니까?
S: 그러면 이 색상은 어떻습니까?
T: 한번 입어보겠습니다.
S: 탈의실은 저쪽에 있습니다.
(잠시 후)
S: 잘 맞습니까?
T: 허리가 너무 끼는군요. 다른 것을 보여주십시오.
S: 알겠습니다. 잠시만 기다려주십시오. 이것은 손님에게 잘 어울릴 것 같습니다.
T: 이것은 꼭 맞습니다.
S: 잘 되었군요. 그밖에 필요한 것은 없습니까?
T: 오늘은 그게 전부 다입니다. 얼마입니까?
S: 75달러입니다.
T: 너무 비싸군요. 할인해주실 수 있습니까?
S: 손님, 이것은 20% 할인된 가격입니다.
T: 그런 여유가 없습니다. 내 예산의 한계는 70달러입니다.
S: 좋습니다. 예외적으로 5%를 추가 할인해 드리겠습니다. 이것이 우리의 최저 가격입니다.
T: 그것을 사겠습니다.
S: 저쪽 카운터에서 계산해주십시오. 고맙습니다.
T: 고맙습니다.

(3) 쇼핑 후 물건의 문제 발생

S: 무엇을 도와드릴까요?
T: 예, 어제 이 카메라를 샀습니다. 그런데 작동을 하지 않는군요. 환불을 받을 수 있습니까?
S: 손님, 죄송합니다. 돈은 환불을 해드리지 않습니다. 같은 가격의 다른 것으로 바꿔 드리겠습니다.
T: 알겠습니다. 다른 것으로 교환하겠습니다.

(4) 편의점에서의 쇼핑

T: 실례하지만 칫솔은 어디서 살 수 있나요?
P: 편의점에서 살 수 있어요.
T: 이 근처에 편의점이 있나요?
P: 예, 저쪽 모퉁이에 세븐일레븐이 있어요.
T: 너무 감사합니다.
(편의점에서)
T: 실례하지만 칫솔은 어디 있지요?
C: 왼쪽으로 5번째 통로에 있어요. 문구류 옆이지요.

(5) 쇼핑 후 선물 포장과 배달

E: 더 필요하신 거 있으세요.
T: 없어요. 그리고 이 선물을 포장하고 싶은데요.
E: 이쪽으로 가지고 오세요.
C: 어떤 포장지로 해드릴까요?
T: 내 아들 생일선물인데, 어떤 포장지가 좋을까요?
C: 이 색은 어떠세요?
T: 좋아요. 그리고 힐튼 호텔까지 배달 좀 해주세요.
C: 알겠습니다.

Chapter 5. 방문과 연극 · 영화 등의 관람

1. 공장 견학

(1) 견학시 주의사항

공장 견학에 대한 안내입니다. 반드시 오전 9시보다 좀 일찍 도착하고, 또한 견학은 정오까지 완료하도록 하겠습니다.

본 공장은 워낙 크기 때문에 여러분들은 걷기 편한 신발을 신으세요. 이 건물은 국방관계의 공장이기 때문에 보안법칙을 지킬 필요가 있으니까 견학하는 분들께 다음 사항을 전해주세요.

① 공장 안에서의 촬영, 카메라 지참은 금지되어 있습니다.
② 카세트 등 그밖의 녹음기구는 금지되어 있습니다.
③ 공장 견학 동안에는 인식용 배지를 달아주세요. 배지는 도착하기 전 준비해 두겠습니다.
④ 두 그룹으로 나누어 각각 가이드를 배정하겠습니다.

각 그룹은 가이드에서 멀어지지 않도록 해주세요. 저희 사무실은 공장 안에 있고, 월요일에 전화를 걸고 싶을 때에는 543-2943번이나 543-2543번으로 걸어주세요. 시카고 직통전화입니다. 자택 전화번호는 743-1832입니다.

용건이 있을 때에는 주저 없이 전화해주세요. 여러분이 오시는 것을 기다리고 있겠습니다.

(2) 공장 방문의 의논에서 견학 순서, 시간, 통지서의 내용을 전화로 재확인

T: 여보세요, 미스터 영 있습니까? 공장장 데이비드 영 말입니다.
O: 예, 있습니다. 이름을 말씀해 주시겠습니까?

T: 김입니다. 사전 예약하는 공장 견학에 대해서 이야기하고 싶습니다.
O: 기다리세요, 미스터 김.
M: 영입니다.
T: 미스터 영입니까? 김입니다. 내일 공장 방문에 대해서 몇 가지 항목을 다시 체크하고 싶습니다.
M: 예. 경민문화관광연구소로부터 내일 아침 당신들이 방문한다는 편지를 받았습니다.
T: 공장에 어떻게 가는지 알려주시겠습니까? 지금 힐튼 호텔에 있습니다.
M: 그렇습니까? 그럼 넬슨 국도로 에반덜 포인트까지 와주세요. 그 교차점의 이정표는 저희 회사의 심벌인 광고가 있는 오래된 지붕이 있는 빌딩입니다.
T: 예.
M: 그리고 왼쪽으로 10분 정도 오면 우측에 저희 공장이 있습니다. 2번 게이트로 들어오세요. 공장에 들어오면 우선 접수처에서 인사부장인 갸농씨와 만나서 그 사람의 지시를 따라주세요.
T: 알겠습니다. 그럼 그쪽에 도착할 시간인데 오전 8:30 이전에 저희들이 도착해야만 한다고 통지서에 쓰여져 있는데 틀림없습니까?.
M: 예, 맞습니다.
T: 그럼 오전 8시쯤 도착하도록 하겠습니다.
M: 미스터 김, 알겠습니다. 그밖의 용건은 없습니까?
T: 좀 문제가 있는데요.
M: 무엇입니까?
T: 오후에 관광하기 위해서 전원 카메라를 가지고 갑니다. 통지서에는 카메라는 일체 안 된다고 되어 있습니다.
M: 문제없습니다. 가지고 오세요. 접수처에 와서 가농씨에게 맡기고 공장견학을 하십시오.
T: 고맙습니다.
M: 천만에요.
T: 통지서에 있는 여타 사항은 단원들이 알고 있습니다. 즉 카세트를 사용하지 말 것, 걷기 편한 구두를 신을 것, 2그룹으로 나누어서 가이드의 지시를 따를 것.
M: 그렇습니다.
T: 미스터 영, 그럼 내일 아침에 만나겠습니다.
M: 전화 감사합니다.

(3) 지인 방문의 확인과 미팅

1) 면회의 약속과 시간 약속

T: 여보세요, 클린트씨. 저는 김이고, 미국을 여행중인 한국인 단체의 인솔자입니다.
S: 그런데 미스터 김, 무슨 용무 있으십니까?
T: 기억하십니까? 저는 작년 겨울 서울에서 PATA 회의에 참석했습니다. 그때 한

국인 여행자가 자주 방문하는 미국의 목적지에 대한 정보를 드리겠다고 약속했습니다.

S: 아, 생각났습니다, 미스터 김. 추운 겨울날 서울의 인사동 식당에서 만났지요. 불고기가 맛있었습니다.

T: 그렇습니다. 보고서를 가지고 왔습니다. 보고서에는 10곳의 미국 목적지와 한국인 관광객 수가 적혀 있습니다.

S: 정말입니까? 감사합니다., 미스터 김.

T: 내일 보고서를 드리려고 생각합니다. 저희들은 여기에서 수일간 체재하기 때문에 내일 점심에는 시간이 있습니다.

S: 공교롭게도 내일 점심은 선약이 있습니다. 내일 오후 6시 이후는 어떻습니까?

T: 7시 반 이후라면 시간이 있습니다. 저녁식사는 어떻습니까? 너무 늦습니까?

S: 7시 반 괜찮습니다. 해밀턴에서 7시 반에 만날까요? 그곳의 소고기 요리는 맛있습니다.

T: 좋습니다, 클린트씨. 그럼 내일 7시 반 해밀턴에서 만납시다. 한국 여행객의 동향에 대해서 내일 이야기합시다.

S: 그렇게 합시다. 그럼 내일 저녁에 만납시다. 전화주셔서 감사합니다.

2. 영화 · 연극 신청시의 회화

(1) 호텔종업원에게 상영영화 및 영화관의 일반적인 사항 문의

H: 안녕하십니까, 무엇을 도와드릴까요?

T: 오늘 저녁 단체로 연극을 보러가고 싶은데 지금 어떤 연극이 상연중인가요? 추천해 주시겠습니까?

H: 예, 이 극장 안내에도 있듯이 브로드웨이 극장에서는 "캣츠"를 상연하고, 또 하나의 극장에서는 "오페라의 유령"을 상연하고 있습니다.

T: 지금 인기 있는 연극은 무엇입니까?

H: "캣츠"입니다.

T: 재미있겠네요. 표는 어디서 구매할 수 있습니까?

H: 극장의 티켓 판매소에서 사실 수 있습니다.

T: 연극은 언제 시작하나요?

H: 4시와 7시에 시작합니다. 1회는 이미 시작했습니다. 7:00부터의 2회 관람하시면 될 것이라고 생각합니다.

T: 감사합니다. 그때쯤에 극장에 가보겠습니다.

(2) 호텔종업원에게 콘서트 좌석 예약 부탁

H: 안녕하십니까, 무엇을 도와드릴까요?

T: 예, 우리는 오늘 저녁에 콘서트를 보려고 합니다. 예약 좀 해주시겠습니까?

H: 예, 손님. 5번가에 있는 브로드웨이 극장에 여러분을 위한 좌석을 예약해 두겠습니다.
T: 극장에서 연주중인 프로그램은 어떤 것이 있습니까?
H: 베토벤 레오노레 서곡 3번, 모차르트 피아노 협주곡 제20번 D단조 K.466, 베토벤 교향곡 제7번 A장조 작품 92번이 연주중입니다.
T: 알겠습니다. 10좌석을 예약해주십시오.
H: 잘 알겠습니다, 손님. 콘서트는 저녁 6시에 시작됩니다.
T: 예, 그런데 극장으로 가는 길을 알려주십시오.
H: 극장의 셔틀버스가 5시 30분에 여러분들을 태우러올 것입니다.
T: 아주 좋습니다.

(3) 인기를 끌고 있는 공연 티켓은 구하기 어렵다. 사전에 수배가 필요하다.

TE: 안녕하십니까, 어떤 표를 원하십니까?
T: 안녕하십니까? "캣츠" 7시 표 30장 부탁합니다.
TE: 오늘 분입니까?
T: 그렇습니다.
TE: 어떤 자리를 원하십니까?
T: 무대 근처 첫줄 좌석 30개를 원합니다.
TE: 죄송합니다만, 오늘은 첫줄은 만석입니다. 오직 뒷줄만 남아 있습니다.
T: 이런, 곤란합니다. 뒷줄은 잘 보이지 않습니다.
TE: 이 연극은 두 달 동안 계속 상영하고 있습니다. 이번주 목요일에 첫줄 자리가 남아 있습니다.
T: 좋습니다. 이번주 목요일 7시 "캣츠" 표 30장 주십시오.
TE: 300달러 되겠습니다.
T: 여기 있습니다.
TE: 표를 확인해보십시오.
T: 예 모두 정확합니다.

(4) 유인기 있는 경기 표는 당일에는 판매하지 않기 때문에 예매를 해야 한다. 한국과 같이 암표상이 나타나기도 한다.

T: 오늘 경기 표를 살 수 있습니까?
TE: 안 됩니다. 매진입니다.
T: 입석도 매진입니까?
TE: 예.
TB: 오늘 경기 표가 있습니다. 필요합니까?
T: 예, 그렇습니다. 얼마면 될까요?
TB: 한 장에 50달러입니다.

T: 너무 비쌉니다. 왜 그렇게 비싸지요?
TB: 그게 장사입니다. 어떻게 하시겠습니까?
T: 사지 않겠습니다.
TB: 매표소는 아침 11시에 엽니다. 줄을 서서 그 다음 날의 표를 사야만 합니다..
T: 그렇습니까? 어쨌든 내일 아침에 와서 표를 사도록 하겠습니다. 알려줘서 고맙습니다.
TB: 천만에요.

Chapter 6. 레스토랑에서

1. 레스토랑의 예약과 주문

(1) 레스토랑의 좌석 예약

R: 안녕하십니까, 아메리칸 르네상스입니다. 무엇을 도와드릴까요?
T: 여보세요, 아메리칸 르네상스지요? 오늘 저녁 7시에 테이블을 예약하고 싶습니다.
R: 몇 분 좌석으로 예약을 해드릴까요?
T: 우리 일행은 30명입니다.
R: 흡연석과 금연석 중 어떤 곳을 원하십니까?
T: 흡연석으로 주십시오.
R: 죄송합니다만 그 시간에는 만석입니다. 8시 이후에나 빈자리가 나올 것 같습니다.
T: 좋습니다. 8시까지 가겠습니다. 그리고 창가에 있는 자리가 되겠습니까?
R: 노력해 보겠습니다. 성함을 말씀해 주시겠습니까?
T: 저는 해피 투어의 인솔자인 김입니다.
R: 8시에 창가 쪽 흡연석 30좌석 예약하셨습니다. 맞습니까?
T: 예, 감사합니다. 양복과 넥타이가 필요합니까?
R: 그렇게 해주시면 감사하겠습니다.
T: 예, 알겠습니다.
R: 전화주셔서 감사합니다, 미스터 김. 8시에 여러분들을 기다리겠습니다.

2. 레스토랑 입구에서

(1) 예약을 했을 때

R: 어서 오십시오. 예약은 하셨습니까?

T: 예, 저는 해피 투어의 미스터 김이고, 30명분을 예약했습니다.
R: 예, 미스터 김. 이리로 오십시오. 창문 옆에 좋은 테이블로 준비해 두었습니다. 이 좌석은 어떠십니까?
T: 아주 좋습니다.
R: 더 오실 분이 계십니까?
T: 아니오, 없습니다. 오직 30명뿐입니다.
R: 알겠습니다. 자리에 앉으십시오. 곧 여기로 담당직원이 올 것입니다.

(2) 예약을 하지 않았을 때

R: 무엇을 도와드릴까요? 예약은 하셨습니까?
T: 아니오, 혹시 30명이 이용할 수 있는 좌석이 있습니까?
R: 지금은 4좌석밖에 없지만 곧 단체석이 나올 것입니다.
T: 얼마나 기다려야 합니까?
R: 약 15분 정도 기다리시면 됩니다. 여기서 잠시만 기다리십시오. 좌석이 나오면 손님의 성함을 부르겠습니다.
T: 좋습니다.
R: 성함이 어떻게 되십니까?
T: 김입니다.

3. 바에서 음료 주문

(1) 음료 주문시(A)

B: 어서 오십시오. 무엇을 드시겠습니까?
T: 위스키 5잔, 스카치 3잔, 맥주 2병, 칵테일 4잔 주십시오.
B: 스카치는 언더락으로 해보시는 것이 어떠십니까?
T: 언더락이란 것은 무엇을 의미합니까?
B: 락은 얼음을 의미합니다. 그래서 그것은 얼음을 갈지 않은 채 그대로 넣은 스트레이트 스카치를 의미합니다.
T: 알겠습니다. 만약 우리가 알코올을 원하지 않는다면 어떤 칵테일을 추천해 주시겠습니까?
B: 백설공주를 추천해 드리겠습니다. 백설공주는 복숭아로 만들었고, 알코올이 없습니다.
T: 좋습니다. 그리고 만약 당신이 주류에 아무것도 넣는 것을 원하지 않는다면 어떻게 해달라고 하겠습니까?
B: "스카치 스트레이트로 주십시오" 또는 "위스키 두 잔을 스트레이트로 주십시오"라고 말하겠습니다.
T: 스카치 한 잔은 언더락으로, 두 잔은 스트레이트로 주시고, 위스키는 두 잔만

스트레이트로 주십시오. 그리고 치즈 크래커 5개와 나쵸 3개를 주십시오. 모두 얼마입니까?

B: 120 달러입니다.

T: 여기에 있습니다.

B: 감사합니다.

(2) 음료 주문시(B)

B: 무엇을 드시겠어요?

T: 과일 주스 있나요?

B: 예, 손님. 오렌지, 토마토, 망고가 있고, 여기서 유명한 '블루 피치'가 있습니다.

T: 블루 피치가 좋을 것 같군요.

B: 예, 다른 필요하신 것은 없으신가요?

T: 다른 사람들은 차가운 맥주를 주세요. 종류가 어떻게 되나요?

B: 칭타오, 기네스와 사포로가 있습니다.

T: 흑맥주는 없나요?

B: 죄송하지만 이 세 종류밖에 없습니다.

T: 좋습니다. 블루 피치 3잔과 칭타오 12병을 주세요.

(3) 음료 주문시(C)

B: 안녕하세요. 저희는 스카치, 데낄라, 아이리쉬, 꼬냑, 럼, 진, 보드카, 캐네디언 리퀴르가 있습니다. 무엇을 드릴까요?

T1: 리퀴르 한 잔 주세요.

B: 손님은요?

T2: 난 데낄라로 주세요.

B: 그리고 안주는 무엇을 하시겠어요?

T: 안주는 필요없는데요.

B: 죄송합니다만 8시 이후부터는 안주를 주문하셔야 합니다.

T: 좋아요. 뭐가 있나요?

B: 칩앤 살사와 치즈스틱앤 소세지가 있습니다.

T: 칩앤 살사를 주세요.

4. 간단한 주문 방법

(1) 식사 주문

R: 안녕하세요, 예약은 하셨습니까?

T: 예, 8시로 예약을 했습니다.

R: 손님의 성함이 어떻게 되십니까?

T: 저는 김입니다.
R: (예약자 명단을 살펴보고) 예. 미스터 김. 여기에 성함이 있습니다. 모두 오셨습니까?
T: 예, 모두 왔습니다.
R: 좋습니다. 제가 여러분의 자리로 안내해 드리겠습니다. 이리로 오십시오. 자리 괜찮으십니까?
T: 예, 아주 좋습니다. 메뉴를 보겠습니다. 주문할 준비가 되면 부르겠습니다.
R: 예, 여기에 있습니다.
(잠시 후)
R: 주문하시겠습니까?
T: 주방장은 어떤 요리를 권합니까?
R: 주방장은 이 코스를 권합니다. 이건 오늘의 특별 요리입니다.
T: 좋습니다. 먹어보겠습니다.
R: 식사 전에 음료수를 드시겠습니까?
T: 예, 적포도주 10잔, 칵테일 13잔, 맥주 7병 부탁합니다.
R: 어떤 종류의 맥주를 드시겠습니까?
T: 맥주 목록을 좀 보여주십시오.
R: 여기 있습니다.
T: 감사합니다. 밀러로 하겠습니다.
R: 에피타이저로 무엇을 드시겠습니까?
T: 새우 칵테일을 선택하겠습니다.
R: 좋습니다. 그리고 수프는 어떻게 하시겠습니까?
T: 버섯 크림 수프 18개와 크랩 검보 12개를 주문하겠습니다.
R: 주요리는 무엇으로 하시겠습니까?
T: 우리 모두 티본 스테이크로 주십시오. 샐러드는 스테이크와 같이 나옵니까?
R: 그렇습니다. 스테이크는 어떻게 드시겠습니까?
T: 중간으로 익혀주십시오.
R: 어떤 드레싱을 드시겠습니까?
T: 사우전드 아일랜드로 주십시오.
R: 무엇을 곁들여 드시겠습니까?
T: 으깬 감자와 새우 프라이를 주십시오.
R: 음료는 어떻게 하시겠습니까?
T: 콜라 10잔, 크림과 설탕을 넣은 커피 15잔, 그리고 나머지는 물을 주십시오.
R: 그밖에 필요한 것은 없으십니까?
T: 디저트로 커스터드 푸딩 15개와 바닐라 아이스크림 15개를 주십시오.
R: 예, 잘 선택하셨습니다. 곧 준비해 드리겠습니다.

(2) 식사 전후의 간단한 음료와 디저트 주문

R: 주문하시겠어요?

T: 조금 뒤에 할게요.
R: 칵테일 먼저 하시겠어요?
T: 예, 블랙러시안으로 주세요.
R: 다른 필요한 것은 없으세요?
T: 커피 주세요.
R: 크림을 넣어드릴까요?
T: 아니오, 그냥 블랙으로 주세요.
(점심식사 후)
R: 디저트는 무엇으로 하시겠어요?
T: 뭐가 있나요?
R: 체리 아이스크림과 모든 종류의 케이크가 있어요.
T: 체리 아이스크림으로 하겠어요. 그리고 레몬을 넣은 홍차도 한잔 주세요.
R: 홍차는 무엇으로 드릴까요?
T: 보통홍차 있나요?
R: 예, 립톤티가 있습니다.
T: 그걸로 할게요.

(3) 패스트푸드점에서의 주문

F: 주문하시겠어요?
T: 예, 치즈버거 5개, 푸렌치 후라이즈 큰걸로 3개, 해쉬포테이토 2개, 콜라 큰걸로 4개 그리고 콜라 작은 거 2개 주세요.
F: 드시고 가시겠어요, 포장하시겠어요?
T: 여기서 먹고 갈 겁니다.
F: 다른 것은 필요없으세요?
T: 없습니다.
F: 치즈버거는 어떻게 해드릴까요?
T: 마요네즈와 겨자를 더 넣어주세요.
F: 알겠습니다. 35달러입니다.
T: 여기 있습니다.
F: 여기 잔돈 있습니다. 주문하신 것은 곧 가져오겠습니다.
T: 그리고 빨대는 어디에 있지요?
F: 저쪽에 있습니다.

5. 레스토랑의 계산

(1) 계산의 전형적인 예

T: 잘 먹었습니다. 맛있었어요.

R: 감사합니다.
T: 계산서를 주시겠습니까?
R: 계산서는 따로따로 드릴까요, 아니면 하나로 드릴까요?
T: 하나로 주십시오.
R: 예. (잠시 후) 총액 계산서입니다.
T: 세금과 서비스 요금이 포함됩니까?
R: 전부 들어 있습니다.
T: 아메리칸 익스프레스 신용카드로 계산해도 되겠습니까?
R: 예, 물론입니다.
T: 여기 있습니다.
R: 여기에 사인 부탁드립니다.
T: 예.
R: 감사합니다. 또 오시길 바랍니다. 안녕히 가십시오.

(2) 식사 후의 계산(A)

R: 저녁식사는 만족스러우셨습니까?
T: 매우 만족스러웠습니다.
R: 여기에 영수증이 있습니다. 모두 252달러입니다. 10%의 봉사요금과 10%의 세금을 포함한 가격입니다.
T: 한국 돈도 받습니까?
R: 물론입니다, 손님.
T: 환율이 어떻게 됩니까?
R: 1달러에 1200원입니다. 환산하면 32만 원입니다.
T: 여기에 35만 원 있습니다.
R: 거스름돈은 한국 돈으로 원하십니까?
T: 아닙니다. 상관없습니다.
R: 여기에 거스름돈과 영수증이 있습니다. 한번 확인해보십시오.
T: 감사합니다.

(2) 식사 후의 계산(B)

R: 식사는 어떠셨어요?
T: 너무 좋았습니다, 감사합니다. 수표로 계산해도 되나요?
R: 죄송합니다만 저희는 개인수표는 받지 않습니다.
T: 알겠어요. 현금으로 계산할게요. 전부 얼마지요?
R: 270달러입니다.
T: 여기 300달러 있습니다.
R: 감사합니다, 손님. 300달러 받았습니다. 여기에 영수증과 잔돈입니다.
T: 참, 테이블에 팁을 두는 것 깜빡했군요.

R: 감사합니다, 하지만 저희는 팁을 받지 않습니다. 10% 봉사료에 팁이 포함되어 있습니다.
T; 아, 그렇군요.
R: 감사합니다. 다시 방문해주세요.

Chapter 7. 각종 문제의 처리

1. 항공기

(1) 항공기의 지연

T: 이 비행기가 2시간 지연되고 있죠, 그렇지요?
A: 죄송합니다. 안개가 너무 심해서 지금 이륙을 할 수가 없습니다.
T: 언제 출발할 수 있지요?
A: 출발 안내방송이 곧바로 나올 겁니다.
T: 만약 이 비행기가 더 지연된다면 전 서울행 연결기를 놓치게 됩니다.
A: 걱정하지 마십시오. 출발 예정시간은 2시 20분입니다.
T: 제발 그렇게 되길 바랍니다.

(2) 항공기 결항

A: 무엇을 도와드릴까요?
T: 뉴욕행 210편 비행기 어떻게 되었습니까?
A: 폭우로 인해 오늘 뉴욕행 210편 비행기는 취소되었습니다.
T: 전 내일 저녁 6시까지는 뉴욕에 도착해야 합니다. 그 시간까지 그곳에 도착하는 다른 비행기가 있습니까?
A: 몇 명이십니까?
T: 우리 일행은 30명입니다. 그리고 뉴욕으로 가는 일반석 표를 기다리고 있습니다.
A: 잠시만 기다리십시오. 필라델피아 국제공항으로 오후 9시 떠나는 비행기가 있어서 30개의 좌석을 예약할 수 있습니다.
T: 현지시간으로 오후 5시가 조금 넘겠군요.
A: 그렇습니다. 필라델피아 국제공항까지 논스톱이고, 도착 예정시간은 현지시간으로 오후 5시 15분입니다. 좌석을 예약하시겠습니까?
T: 예, 제 이름은 김이고, 그룹명은 해피 투어입니다.
A: 알겠습니다. 손님 일행의 탑승편은 212편이며, 저녁 9시에 출발하므로 7시까지는 공항으로 나와주십시오. 전화주셔서 감사합니다.

(3) 긴급 착륙에 대비

1) 긴급 착륙에 대비한 문장

① 산소 마스크는 필요에 따라 머리 위의 선반에서 자동적으로 제공됩니다. 핀이 떨어질 때까지 당겨주세요 마스크에 넣어져 있는 호스와 흡입주머니를 제거해주세요

② 그대로 좌석을 떠나지 말아주세요 담배는 피우지 마세요. 불붙인 담배는 즉시 꺼주세요. 지금 당장 가까이 있는 마스크를 집어 얼굴에 대주세요. 마스크를 당기면 산소가 호스를 따라 흘러나옵니다.

③ 마스크를 바로 코와 입어 대주세요. 산소 공급 튜브는 좌석에서 천천히 흡입할 수 있을 만큼의 길이입니다. 아동용으로 예비마스크가 각 열에서 사용할 수 있도록 되어 있습니다.

④ 구명구의 양옆에 붙어 있는 조임쇠를 몸에 붙여주세요. 구명구를 부풀리기 위해서는 빨간 손잡이를 강하게 당깁니다. 더 부풀리고 싶을 때는 입을 사용합니다. 단 기내에서는 부풀리지 말아주세요.

⑤ 비상용 도어를 열기 위해서는 핸들을 시계 반대방향으로 돌리고 밖으로 밀어 냅니다. 탈출용 미끄럼틀이 자동적으로 나옵니다.

⑥ 높은 상공에서는 난기류가 심합니다. 좌석 벨트의 사인이 비행중에 들어왔을 때에는 그 사인에 따라 벨트를 매지 않으면 부상의 염려가 있습니다.

⑦ 여행에 익숙한 여행자는 좌석 벨트를 느슨하게 매고, 벨트 사인이 들어왔을 때에는 조여주세요.

⑧ 출구가 어디인지 잘 기억해주세요. 특히 당신 좌석에서 가장 가까운 출구가 필요합니다. 그리고 문을 여는 방법도 기억해두세요.

⑨ 불시착자세-구두를 벗고 안경은 벗고, 뾰족한 물건을 주머니에서 꺼내고 방어적인 자세를 취해주세요.

⑩ 비행기에서 탈출할 때 코트류, 핸드백 등을 들지 말아주세요. 곧바로 출구 쪽으로 탈출하는 겁니다.

⑪ 탈출 미끄럼틀로 뛰어듭니다. 미끄럼틀을 손으로 집어서는 안 됩니다. 비행기 창으로부터 뛰어나올 때에는 한쪽 발을 먼저 내고, 다음으로 머리를, 그 다음에 어깨 순으로 나옵니다.

2) 불시착할 때의 기장 아나운스와 주의사항

(기장의 아나운스는 승객에게 불안을 주지 않는 것이 중요하다)

저는 기장입니다. 잘 들어주세요. 엔진이 고장났으므로 수분 후에 긴급 착륙하게 됩니다만 염려하지 마십시오. 좌석 벨트를 매고, 그대로 좌석을 떠나지 말아주세요. 탑승기가 안전하게 멈춘 후에는 승무원의 지시에 따라주세요.

2. 귀중품의 분실

(1) 분실한 화물을 찾아달라는 의뢰

T: 실례합니다, 경찰관 아저씨.
P: 무엇을 도와드릴까요?
T: 우리 일행 중 한 명이 가방을 잃어버렸습니다.
P: 언제, 어디서 잃어버렸습니까?
T: 30분 전 8번가에서 버스를 기다리는 도중에 잃어버렸습니다.
P: 가방 안에는 무엇이 있었습니까?
T: 여행자 수표, 신용카드, 여권, 그리고 500달러가 있었습니다.
P: 분실 신고서를 작성하여 주십시오. 발견하는 대로 연락하겠습니다.
T: 우리는 이번 주말까지 힐튼 호텔에 머물 예정입니다. 발견되는 대로 호텔에 가져다주십시오.

(2) 여권을 분실하였을 때

T: 실례합니다. 한국대사관 가는 길을 알려 주시겠습니까?
P: 예, 곧장 가셔서 두번째 모퉁이에서 왼쪽으로 돌면 한국 국기를 볼 수 있습니다.
T: 감사합니다.
E: 무엇을 도와드릴까요?
T: 여권을 분실하였습니다. 그것을 재발급받고 싶습니다.
E: 언제, 어디서 분실하셨습니까?
T: 오후 1시경 지하철에서 잃어버린 것 같습니다.
E: 이 서식에 기재해주시고, 잠시만 기다리세요.

(3) 신용카드 분실시 신고할 때

C: 마스터 카드사입니다. 무엇을 도와드릴까요?
T: 제 신용카드를 잃어버렸습니다.
C: 걱정하지 마세요. 이름과 카드번호를 말씀해주세요.
T: 제 이름은 김이고, 카드번호는 기억할 수가 없습니다.
C: 문제없습니다. 카드 사용을 정지시키겠습니다. 확인되었으니 재발행해 드리겠습니다.
T: 감사합니다.

3. 의사를 부를 때

(1) 환자가 생겼을 때 의사가 오기까지 해야 할 응급처치에 대한 회화

O: 예. 교환입니다.
T: 1106호입니다. 객실 투숙객 중 한 명이 몸이 안 좋은 것 같습니다. 호텔 전용 의사가 있습니까?
O: 예, 어떤 증상이 있습니까?
T: 열이 아주 심합니다.
O: 알겠습니다. 내과의사를 곧 보내 드리겠습니다. 지금 시간은 곧 올 수 있을 겁니다.
T: 휴, 다행이군요. 그리고 아스피린과 체온계는 어디서 살 수 있을까요?
O: 지하 약국에서 판매하고 있습니다.
(약국에서)
C: 무엇을 도와드릴까요?
T: 아스피린 몇 알과 체온계를 주십시오.
C: 예, 잠시만 기다리세요. 여기에 있습니다.
T: 이 약을 몇 알 먹어야 합니까?
C: 한 알씩 드십시오.
T: 체온계는 어떻게 사용해야 합니까?
C: 여기의 체온계는 화씨이므로 섭씨로 하기 위해서는 32를 빼고 5를 곱해서 9로 나눠야 합니다. 그리고 구강용입니다.
T: 한국에서는 겨드랑이에 넣습니다. 습관이란 것이 나라마다 다르군요.

(2) 건강 관리실

D: 어디가 아프십니까?
T: 배가 아프다고 합니다.
D: 언제부터 아팠습니까?
T: 오늘 아침식사 후부터 아팠다고 합니다.
D: 무엇을 먹었습니까?
T: 치킨, 과일 햄 그리고 우유를 먹었다고 합니다.
D: 설사는 있었습니까?
T: 예.
D: (진찰 후) 걱정하지 마십시오. 소화불량일 뿐입니다. 이 처방전을 약국에 가지고 가십시오.
T: 감사합니다.

4. 교통사고를 신고할 때

T: 여보세요, 911이지요?
E: 예, 무엇을 도와드릴까요?
T: 교통사고가 났습니다. 앰뷸런스를 보내주세요.
E: 운전자이십니까?
T: 아닙니다. 저는 한국에서 온 인솔자입니다. 우리 일행이 워싱턴 다리에서 사진을 찍고 있는데, 갑자기 트럭이 뒤에서 치고 달아났습니다.
E: 알겠습니다. 곧 가겠습니다.
T: 서둘러 주시겠어요? 매우 위급한 상황입니다.
E: 다치셨습니까?
T: 예, 저는 팔이 부러졌습니다. 우리 일행 중 한 명은 머리에서 피가 나오고 있고, 의식을 잃었습니다. 3명은 입에서 피가 흐르고 있습니다.
E: 심각한 상황이군요. 침착하십시오.
T: 알겠습니다. 얼마나 기다려야 하나요?
E: 2분 뒤에 도착할 것입니다.

5. 호텔 객실에서의 문제 해결

T: 객실담당 부탁합니다.
H: 객실담당입니다. 무엇을 도와드릴까요?
T: 707호실입니다. 호텔 시설에 대해서 묻고 싶습니다.
H: 손님, 무슨 문제라도 있으십니까?
T: 내 객실 말인데요. 이렇게 지저분한 객실은 처음 봅니다. 도대체 이것이 무슨 일입니까?
H: 죄송합니다. 곧 사람을 보내겠습니다. 객실의 문제점을 정확히 말씀해 주시겠습니까?
T: 침대는 정리가 안 되어 있고, 욕조는 불결합니다.
H: 알겠습니다.
T: 변기는 지저분하고, 물도 내려가지 않습니다. 게다가 하수구도 막혔습니다.
H: 알겠습니다. 욕실과 객실이 모두 손님들이 사용하기에는 적합하지 않다는 말씀이시지요.
T: 정확히 맞습니다.
H: 정말 죄송합니다. 프런트 데스크와 객실담당 부서의 착오로 인하여 청소를 하도록 표시해둔 객실을 손님께 드린 것 같습니다. 곧 정리된 방을 드리겠습니다.
T: 그렇게 되길 바랍니다.

Chapter 8. 통신과 환전

1. 전 화

(1) 교환에게서 컬렉트콜 전화를 받는다

O: 교환입니다. 무엇을 도와드릴까요?
T: 한국으로 국제전화를 하고 싶습니다. 컬렉트콜로 부탁합니다.
O: 전화번호는 몇 번입니까?
T: 02-555-6481입니다.
O: 누구에게 전화하시겠습니까?
T: 미스터 최에게요.
O: 댁의 성함과 전화번호는 어떻게 됩니까?
T: 저는 김이고, 전화번호는 714-865-7528입니다.
O: 잠시만 기다리세요. (미스터 최. 미스터 김으로부터 컬렉트콜입니다. 받으시겠습니까?) 미스터 김, 전화 연결되었습니다. 통화하세요.
T: 감사합니다.

(2) 외부에서 호텔로 걸려온 전화

O: 안녕하세요, 힐튼 호텔입니다. 무엇을 도와드릴까요?
C: 1752호의 미스터 송과 통화하고 싶습니다.
O: 잠시만 기다리세요. 죄송합니다만, 미스터 송은 방에 안 계십니다. 메시지 남겨드릴까요?
C: 예, 미스터 최가 전화했다고 전해 주시겠습니까?
O: 알겠습니다. 손님의 전화번호가 어떻게 되십니까?
C: 그가 제 번호를 알고 있습니다.
O: 예, 제가 미스터 송에게 메시지를 전달해 드리겠습니다.
C: 감사합니다.

(3) 외부에서 호텔로 잘못 걸려온 전화

O: 하얏트 호텔입니다. 무엇을 도와드릴까요?
D: 예, 9257호에 있는 미스터 김을 부탁합니다.
O: 잠시만 기다리세요. 죄송하지만 미스터 김은 저희 호텔 손님이 아닙니다.
D: 이럴 수가요. 그가 여기로 전화하라고 했는데요. 다시 한번 확인해주세요.
O: 예, 손님. 죄송하지만 저희 객실 어디에도 미스터 김은 없습니다.
D: 거기 6235-7248 아닌가요?
O: 죄송합니다만 잘못 거셨어요. 여기는 6235-7240이에요.

D: 아, 제가 실수했군요. 귀찮게 해서 죄송합니다.
O: 괜찮습니다.

2. 우체국에서의 회화

(1) 소포를 부칠 때

P: 안녕하십니까, 무엇을 도와드릴까요?
T: 소포는 어느 창구에서 취급하고 있습니까?
P: 여기에서 하고 있습니다.
T: 이 소포를 서울에 보내고 싶습니다.
P: 어떻게 보내시겠습니까?
T: 항공편으로 부탁합니다.
P: 안에 무엇이 들어 있습니까?
T: 앨범과 잡지입니다.
P: 한국 세관은 포르노 심사가 늘 엄한 것 같습니다. 누드는 전혀 허락하지 않는다고 들었습니다.
T: 소포 안에는 포르노 잡지는 들어 있지 않습니다.
P: 이 카드는 수출 신고서입니다. 세관 신고를 해야 합니다. 이 양식에 기입해주십시오.
T: 예, 한국까지 소포요금은 얼마입니까?
P: 운송료가 파운드당 70센트입니다. 무게를 재봅시다. 저기 저울에 올려놓으세요. 7달러 50센트입니다.
T: 여기 있습니다. 그리고 항공 봉함엽서 2장과 우편엽서 5장을 주십시오.
P: 모두 10달러 40센트입니다.
T: 한국에 며칠이면 도착합니까?
P: 약 5일 걸립니다.
T: 알겠습니다. 그리고 이 소포를 보험에 들고 싶습니다.

(2) 편지를 부칠 때

T: 이 편지를 등기우편으로 보내고 싶습니다.
P: 어디로 보내실 거죠?
T: LA로요. 얼마짜리 우표를 붙여야 하나요?
P: 일반크기의 편지입니까?
T: 예, 아주 가벼워요.
P: 3달러 75센트어치를 붙여야 합니다.
T: 속달로 붙이면 어떻게 되죠?
P: 그러면 6달러가 더 듭니다.

3. 은행에서 환전할 때

T: 돈은 어디서 바꿀 수 있습니까?
S: 저를 따라오세요. 안내해드리겠습니다.
T: 감사합니다.
B: 무엇을 도와드릴까요?
T: 환전을 하고 싶습니다.
B: 어떻게 원하세요?
T: 환율이 어떻게 되죠?
B: 1달러에 1200원입니다.
T: 100달러를 20불짜리 3매, 10불짜리 3매, 5불짜리 1매, 그리고 1불짜리 5매를 원합니다.
B: 좋습니다. 여권을 주세요.
T: 여기에 있습니다.
B: 잠시만 기다리십시오. 이 양식을 기재해주시고, 여기에 서명해주세요. 여기서 돈을 확인해주세요.

투어 에스코트 영어

2판 1쇄 발행 2009년 2월 20일

저 자 배 찬·김정욱
발행인 남 승 우

발행처 남두도서
서울특별시 동작구 사당3동 220-43
TEL : (02) 595-1692~4
FAX : (02) 595-1394
E-mail : namdoo6@unitel.co.kr
신고 : 5-76호 (1998. 11. 4)

정가 17,000 원

ISBN 978-89-5780-096-6 93740